AROUND THE TABLE

AROUND THE TABLE

Women on Food, Cooking, Nourishment, Love . . .
and the Mothers Who Dished It Up for Them

LELA NARGI

Foreword by Darra Goldstein

EDITOR, *Gastronomica*

JEREMY P. TARCHER/PENGUIN
a member of Penguin Group (USA) Inc.
New York

JEREMY P. TARCHER/PENGUIN
Published by the Penguin Group
Penguin Group (USA) Inc., 375 Hudson Street, New York, New York 10014, USA •
Penguin Group (Canada), 10 Alcorn Avenue, Toronto, Ontario M4V 3B2, Canada (a division
of Pearson Penguin Canada Inc.) • Penguin Books Ltd, 80 Strand, London WC2R 0RL,
England • Penguin Ireland, 25 St Stephen's Green, Dublin 2, Ireland (a division of Penguin
Books Ltd) • Penguin Group (Australia), 250 Camberwell Road, Camberwell, Victoria 3124,
Australia (a division of Pearson Australia Group Pty Ltd) • Penguin Books India Pvt Ltd,
11 Community Centre, Panchsheel Park, New Delhi–110 017, India • Penguin Group (NZ),
Cnr Airborne and Rosedale Roads, Albany, Auckland 1310, New Zealand (a division of Pearson
New Zealand Ltd) • Penguin Books (South Africa) (Pty) Ltd, 24 Sturdee Avenue,
Rosebank, Johannesburg 2196, South Africa

Penguin Books Ltd, Registered Offices:
80 Strand, London WC2R 0RL, England

Library of Congress Cataloging-in-Publication Data

Nargi, Lela.
Around the table : women on food, cooking, nourishment, love . . . and
the mothers who dished it up for them / Lela Nargi
p.   cm.
ISBN 1-58542-411-0
1. Cookery.   I. Title.
TX651.N35   2005   2004063761
641.5—dc22

Printed in the United States of America
1   3   5   7   9   10   8   6   4   2

Book design by Gretchen Achilles

Most Tarcher/Penguin books are available at special quantity discounts for bulk purchase for
sales promotions, premiums, fund-raising, and educational needs. Special books or book ex-
cerpts also can be created to fit specific needs. For details, write Penguin Group (USA) Inc.
Special Markets, 375 Hudson Street, New York, NY 10014.

The recipes contained in this book are to be followed exactly as written. The publisher
is not responsible for your specific health or allergy needs that may require medical supervi-
sion. The publisher is not responsible for any adverse reactions to the recipes contained in
this book.

While the author has made every effort to provide accurate telephone numbers and In-
ternet addresses at the time of publication, neither the publisher not the author assumes any
responsibility for errors, or for changes that occur after publication. Further, the publisher
does not have any control over and does not assume any responsibility for author or third-
party websites or their content.

For my mother,
who taught me how to love food and cooking

And for Ada,
who I love even more than food and cooking

CONTENTS

FOREWORD

Opening *Around the Table*, I expected just another pleasant read—more culinary tales to enjoy and then forget. Instead, I found myself drawn into a community of women who captivated me with their stories and allowed me to enter into their lives. *Around the Table* is an intimate collection, one that doesn't just celebrate the pleasures of food but shows the pain food can cause. What we eat may unite us, but it can also mark us as Other. Food may nourish, but it can also feed anger and distress. In this collection we see how diet can cause rejection (the stigma of being fat) and anxiety (the anguish of feeding a child ill with cancer), and yet what emerges at the end is a realization that food is the great connector. Apart from moments of guilty pleasure, food is meant to be shared, not taken in isolation.

This book, then, is about relationships. By thinking about food, the women in this collection have come to terms with what has been lost in their lives as well as what has been gained. Their stories introduce us to many different cultures and recreate past worlds. While these kitchen conversations seem to be about food, they are really about life, and they allow us to see just how deeply food resonates with meaning. Gertrude Stein said, "Nothing is more interesting than that something that you eat." *Around the Table* reminds us why this is so. The women in this collection explore not just what they eat but how and why they eat it, and they do so with disarming honesty. They leave us with the certainty that we must once again devote time to sitting around our tables—for kitchen conversations are one of the best ways to create community, whether among family, or neighbors, or out in the larger world.

—DARRA GOLDSTEIN

Editor, *Gastronomica*

AROUND THE TABLE

INTRODUCTION

In the inside there is sleeping, in the outside there is reddening, in the morning there is
meaning, in the evening there is feeling.

"Roastbeef" from *Tender Buttons*
GERTRUDE STEIN

Like many women I know, I lead parallel lives. None of these lives is better or
worse, more or less, than the others. There is no particular order to their relevance to the whole, to the person who is me: writer, mother, wife, cook, eater. But
remove one of these pieces and the whole collapses. Each piece is essential. Each
piece bolsters and informs the others.

I am not *more* a person who cooks and loves to eat than I am a person who writes
and loves to be a wife and mother. I spend a lot of time thinking about food, though:
when I am very hungry, what I can throw together to eat right now; when I am not
so hungry, what I can prepare to eat that is perfect for this particular day, its heat or
bluster, my mood; when I am in the mood to cook for others, what will be interesting to them and challenging for me. Is this surprising, or unnatural? I am a person
who lives in the so-called First World, and so, out of habit and because I can (never
mind my own desire), I eat three meals a day plus snacks. Food punctuates every
morning, afternoon, evening. How can it *not* be almost perpetually on my mind?

It is certainly on the minds of the women in this book.

These are women with a lot on their minds *besides* food, women who, in addition to calling themselves cooks and food enthusiasts and (in many instances) wives and/or mothers, are musicians, mathematicians, marketers; agents, activists, academics; biologists and book editors. In other words, busy women who might be expected to forgo cooking altogether in the interest of always-short time. And yet here they are in the kitchen, in the evening after work, or first thing in the morning before work, or late at night before bed, or all day Saturday or Sunday before the onset of the week's chaos, preparing meals for themselves and their families and their friends. Not out of any sense of womanly, wifely duty, but because they enjoy the process of it, and the end result of it, and recognize the relevance in ever more quick and complicated times of eating "real" food, of sharing a home-cooked meal with those who mean the most to us in our lives. In such a small, simple act lies everything that is important: patience; creativity; time alone; time with others; nourishment, both physical and spiritual; a transference of care and affection in a way that is palpable.

How do you become a woman who enjoys cooking and eating? There is no single formula, although a model for it—positive or negative—certainly helps. In my case, the model is my mother, who has cooked her way through the cuisines of France, Italy, Japan, China, and her own imagination. Food punctuates my past as well as my present; I have few memories of my mother during my childhood that don't involve food in some way. My mother slow-braising a leg of lamb in the electric skillet for Sunday dinner. My mother wrapping candied almonds in white napkins as party favors for my seventh birthday, tying the parcels with blue yarn. My mother talking to me over a dice of onions. My mother laughing with me above a piping of purple icing violets. My mother answering me from beside a shelf of cookbooks, my favorite of which was always the folio of Japanese recipe cards, in whose vividly colored photographs food looked like treasure: carrots carved like swans, sliced fish rolled into roses, grains of rice gleaming like seed pearls. "Food is magic," the photos seemed to whisper. I believed it, in large part, I think, because it seemed my mother believed it. And that was the beginning of everything. Not only of my love for cooking and eating but also for reading about food and, of course, talking about it.

The women who talk about cooking and eating on the pages of this book came to enjoy these pastimes in a variety of ways, for a multitude of reasons. But although these women have different stories to tell, they are all related in one manner or another. Some of them are related by blood or marriage, some by heritage, some by profession, some merely by demeanor. And each one is related to the others by one very distinctive trait: when encouraged to contemplate cooking and eating, they manage to pass time swiftly and poignantly. One memory leads easily to another, and to another, and so on, until a picture of a complete life is composed, with food as its thread.

This book is a roundtable of sorts, with fifteen different yet alike women seated side by side by side and nudged (though not much nudging was necessary) into dialogue, at first only with me—the pieces that appear here are compiled mostly from one-on-one interviews, or, in a few instances, were written in response to an ongoing correspondence with me about food—but in the end, also with each other. The result is a giant conversation, about cooking and food and family and all the minutiae inherent in a life. Recipes are shared, techniques compared; remembrances drift, then harden into matters of practicality; one woman's concerns are the same as, similar to, nothing like another's. I discover pieces of myself in the musings of these women, and at this writing, pulling this project to a close, I consider the ways in which I have been inspired these past months by the things that inspire them: wine roasts and risottos, homemade chicken stocks, tiny lettuces, farmers markets, new ingredients, simplicity, complexity, and, above all, community. They remind me of what I like to cook, and how and why, even though I didn't think I had forgotten. As I remember, the dialogue that is seemingly set here broadens, leading to ever more thoughts and remembrances, giving them new life, ever-evolving meaning.

KATHY EBEL

Screenwriter

I come from a long line of marzipan eaters. Both sides of my mother's family were helmed by industrialist, Jewish patriarchs who ran successful family businesses that employed entire German towns—metals on the one side, fats and oils on the other—towns that were eventually bombed flat. My grandparents' generation was sheltered by its money. They didn't have to be go-getters, since their parents and grandparents had already taken care of business in a big way. This crowd of eight siblings had been groomed to helm a highly polished formal living room, chatting, playing clever parlor games, and eating marzipan. If you've ever seen Vittorio De Sica's film *The Garden of the Finzi-Continis*, you've practically been inside my grandparents' sprawling Berlin apartment where, if Hitler hadn't come along and ruined everything, you could probably find me right now, paring slice after slice of bittersweet chocolate-covered marzipan with a mother-of-pearl inlaid knife engraved with my grandmother's monogram.

I'm always slightly taken aback when I hear others decry marzipan as totally disgusting. I love the stuff. As a kid I favored the trompe l'oeil shapes: fried eggs and sausage, fruits, and whimsical animals. Soon after college, I remember polishing off an enormous plain log of marzipan with my cousins: we just kept slicing until it was gone. These days I eat far fewer sweets—I need them less than I used to—but I will give an affectionate glance to any marzipan displays that cross my path. Somehow, they sum up my family history. So pretty, so artful, so tender with their vegetable coloring, but often melancholy, half-forgotten. They beckon me to buy and to eat, admonish me to remember.

My parents were German-Jewish émigrés, and consummately urban English professors. They knew the Trillings; they had slept in castles, the guests of anti-Semitic Englishmen who granted them a carefully considered exception; they rejected the Germanic plum compotes and pickled herring of their forebears and instead, as newlyweds, cooked oxtail soup and experimented with making their own beer in the bathtub. They got married at twenty-one, my mother ignoring my father's warning that he didn't want children, and split up shortly after my arrival. On the cusp of thirty, my mother was floating around the early 1970s on the wrong side of the Hudson River with a toddler in tow. And here we come to my own Proustian madeleine, which was actually a green whipped-cream frog. This was some time around 1970, in the respectable but modest Teaneck, New Jersey, Colonial-style house for which my parents had inexplicably left Manhattan.

My mother didn't have a car in those days, perhaps a hint that she was hoping to return to the City. I can't imagine who stayed with me that afternoon while my mother trotted off on the half-hour walk to the nicest bakery on Cedar Lane—it's not unlikely that she left me alone. Through a pale midday light, tinged slightly with the fragrance of the lilacs that climbed outside my second-floor bedroom window, and from behind the feverish curtain of one of my first flus, my mother entered my bedroom bearing a small white box tied with candy-striped string. Inside it was a leaf green pastry, airbrushed to resemble the kind of smiling froggie you'd find perched on a cartoon lily pad. I was delighted and gobbled him down according to my own precise logic: using my teeth to lick and peel away the exterior frosting, then nibbling the cake interior, all the while working from the bottom up and saving the head with its buggy yellow frosting eyes for last. And then, just moments later, I projectile vomited a foamy, froggie spray. My mother was utterly surprised. The froggie was a tasty Band-Aid for the bullet wound of the divorce, and the marriage before that, and her own depressive childhood before that, and the war before that. It was supposed to make things better—how could it have made things worse?

The moment is a metaphor, of course, for life with my mother in that era, a time when her intentions and her values existed in a parallel universe to her decisions, and when whipped-cream treats occupied one end of a pendulum that swung along a dark arc. Only I had the full picture of my mother's behind-the-scenes anguish and self-destruction. Isolated by her mostly well-hidden and troubled personal life, my mother's close friendships were performances, special occasions, when she was her best self and I was her precocious child. At home, just the two of us, I was my mother's witness, judge, and confidante, and mealtimes were quiet, charged, and melancholic.

The image of the slim single girl of the time was epitomized by the contents of my mother's sparse pantry: Alba 77 powdered shake mix, cantaloupes poised to be halved and scooped full of Breakstone's low-fat cottage cheese with pineapple, six-packs of Tab. She didn't cook as much as rustle us up a bite to eat from whatever she found in the cabinets. I ate her meals with little complaint, enjoying her lasagna—a terrine of noodles sandwiched with low-fat cottage cheese, stacked in a battered supermarket loaf pan and drenched in bottled tomato sauce—that collapsed in a puddle of watery curd upon serving. I smothered her wet iceberg lettuce and whole cherry tomato salad in creamy bottled dressing, then devoured it.

But what troubled me, even as a small child, were the haphazard details of her kitchen: the uncovered pots of leftovers grown solid in the fridge; ancient condiments with gummy lids askew, forgotten in its door; her ubiquitous pint of Chivas Regal, hidden halfheartedly. But I had my hooch, too: supermarket mother lodes of M&M's and Hershey's Miniatures, and white paper bags of red and black raspberry-shaped gummy fruits from Manhattan candy shops, hidden nearby her own stash. When my mother felt the urge to nurture with food, she did it with sweets.

My mother presented them magically. The heart-shaped box filled with Smarties from a trip to London was left by my bedside to greet me on the morning of Valentine's Day. The marzipan-filled Mozart Kugel was tucked into my jacket pockets ("For later, when you're feeling sad," she would say). Sweets were a more reliable kind of mother love, and I craved them and crammed them, ripping the foil off the next one before the one in my mouth had fully dissolved.

My parents had been part of a cocky, intellectual circle at Columbia University, where they had attended college and graduate school, and after the divorce my mother retained a small circle of family friends who remembered my father as an intellectual star and who shared my mother's bafflement over the gradual psychic implosion that destroyed his career and his reputation and caused him to reject fatherhood along with the rest of his relationships. These households became surrogates for my own, and I immersed myself in our visits with anthropological zeal, observing fathers in action; siblings on the perpetual seesaw of collaboration and betrayal; bossy, exacting mothers who attended consciousness-raising groups but still ran their well-organized households like proper matriarchs. Here, mealtimes were planned, festive, and nurturing. Food was self-expression and family culture. Signature recipes and fresh ingredients were points of pride. Children had their place at these meals. They were sometimes fed separately, with a simpler version of the adult main event. They were admonished to drink their milk. Dessert was a rare treat, not a second course. Furiously, I socked away these images so that I could nibble at them later, concocting an array of orderly new lives to which my mother could shepherd me, if only I could organize our escape route.

I adored our visits to the Applebaums in western Massachusetts, where my mother took me several times a year. There was a tacit understanding all around that we were seeking respite from her disastrous, violent second marriage, to an unemployed, blue-eyed Jewish playboy with an eighth-grade education. His name was rarely mentioned during our visits, allowing me to pretend that he had evaporated.

Ben Applebaum was a Brooklyn-born novelist and UMass English professor; Jenny was from the Midwest, a shiksa watercolorist Ben had met in grad school who had learned the requisite Friday-night Sabbath prayers, and even went so far as to wear a lace schmatte on her head for candle lighting. Their domestic utopia was headquartered in a nineteenth-century parson's house that had a sledding hill in front and an arboretum in back. Faded Oriental carpets made a patchwork on the wooden floors; chilly bathrooms featured claw-footed tubs and colorful towels covered in psychedelic butterflies. The Applebaums had framed black-and-white photographs of Hasidic men at the Wailing Wall, art deco lamps, and three blond children with biblical names, and they loved to cook.

The Applebaums also had a big eat-in kitchen, with a sliding glass door that led to the vegetable garden and another door that opened into their high-raftered barn-cum-garage. They would prepare meals with fresh-picked broccoli, eggplant, yellow and green squash from their garden, a cookbook or two open nearby but receiving only cursory glances, all the while laughingly telling tales of the tripe dish they'd mistakenly ordered when Ben was on sabbatical in France. Their banter, peppered with academic phrases ("conspicuous consumption," "Marshall McLuhan," "A.B.D.") and Nixon jokes, felt familiar to me. But seeing a husband and wife running a house together, creating their own aesthetic universe—this was new and wildly desirable.

Ben cooked for the kids, and his signature dish was spaghetti from a green box with a yellow motif on it, boiled almost to the gummy point then drained, returned to the pot, and tossed with a wedge of salted butter and a thick stream of ketchup. Then he stirred the mess up and added a little more salt. The resulting dish was slick, salty, pink, and sweet, with only the faintest flavor of tomatoes, and served with tall glasses of cold milk. It tasted delicious to me, flavored by the happy milieu and the safety that I felt within it. This was how life was supposed to be—with parents in charge and kids at their own table. Just a few years later, the Applebaums would split in a nasty divorce, but when I needed them most, they provided me with what I understood at the time to be a happy, if temporary, home.

When I was in kindergarten, my mother and I moved from our airy house in integrated Teaneck, where we had some friends nearby, to a small, dark house on an unpaved street in class-obsessed Tenafly, where we knew no one and I was officially miserable. My elementary school did not have a lunch program as much as a lunch detention—a small cluster of tables arranged in the gym, overseen by a round-robin of clucking volunteers, a reluctant concession to working mothers. At the end of one such table, I would unwrap my lunch. This was a noisy production number revealing a warm, squashed mess. By the time I got to the goods, I was the laughingstock.

My mother fashioned her peanut butter and jelly sandwiches from chunky Shop Rite brand peanut butter and thick-cut orange marmalade spread on seeded Levy's Jewish rye bread. She sliced the sandwich in half and wrapped it in a wide swath of wax paper, then sealed the paper with a few strips of masking tape, as though the sandwich were destined for a journey around the tip of Cape Horn via schooner. She would then take a brown paper supermarket bag and cut it with a pair of scissors about five inches up from the bottom, creating a trough. The sandwich got tucked into a corner of the trough, along with a thermos of warm orange juice made from frozen concentrate and tap water, a sentimental handwritten note, a Golden Delicious apple, and a paper napkin. My mother folded the sides of the trough and rolled the entire contraption until the lunch was contained within a package that would then be sealed yet again with masking tape.

One lunch period, I laboriously unwrapped a sandwich of a different filling. This time, it was my mother's tuna salad, gouged from the can too quickly to form flakes. Instead, fairly large hunks of tuna had been given a shake or two of garlic salt and quickly forked through with a dollop of Hellmann's mayonnaise. This was a far cry from the smooth tuna salad of delis and diners, and perhaps why tuna salad was one of the first dishes I learned how to make for myself. As a latchkey child, alone in the afternoons, I had the chance to experiment with cooking. My tuna salad was exceptionally blended and spreadable, carefully flaked from the can into a stainless steel bowl, then minced thoroughly with a fork. Over the years, I would experiment with paper-thin slices of Granny Smith apple, finely chopped scallions, garlic dill pickles, an array of mustards, and even green grapes and pistachios (not all at once, of course, because that would be disgusting). I eventually arrived at my standard: a handful of finely diced celery, a spoonful of Dijon mustard, a spoonful of sweet pickle relish, salt and freshly ground pepper, the occasional pinch of freshly chopped mixed herbs, and only then a dollop of mayonnaise—preferably Trader Joe's Real Mayonnaise, which has an eggy, vinegary, not-too-sweet flavor and a homemade, dressing-like consistency.

On this life-changing day in fourth grade, however, I peeled back the masking tape, unrolled the trough, removed the wax-paper package, peeled back the tape from that, and frowned briefly at the thick, soaked-through sandwich. Pale, scrawny Gloria Lyons, however, peered through her dishwater blond bangs and over at my sandwich with interest. It seemed she wanted to trade.

Gloria Lyons's Oscar Mayer ham and American cheese on white bread with a lone leaf of iceberg lettuce and a substantial schmear of Miracle Whip was a revelation. The bread, the cheese, the spread, and the lettuce were so sweet. And the ham was so . . . hammy. Let me tell you: Nobody loves swine more than a nice Jewish girl. That evening, I shared my news of culinary/entrepreneurial success with my mother. "I traded my lunch today with Gloria Lyons," I reported.

"Oh, how wonderful!" she replied sunnily from behind her *New York Review of Books*. "What did she bring?"

"Ham and cheese on white bread," I replied. A black cloud rolled over my mother's face as she cast aside her reading to glare at me with crushing disappointment and disbelief.

"Ham and cheese!" she cried. "What on earth are you doing eating ham and cheese? We're kosher."

"We are?" I asked, completely confused. This was the first I'd ever heard of it.

Like my parents before me, my husband and I have pursued simple food adventures as a way of defining our collective personal style. While my parents brewed beer in the bathtub, John and I met at a dim sum brunch on a September afternoon in 1995. Ten years later we still enjoy prowling our extended neighborhood for cheap, festive eats, then wowing our friends with our discoveries.

It took me a long time to realize that John is quite shy. When we first met in a massive Chinese banquet hall among a noisy sea of carts, he was on fire. I will never forget how he responded to my disappointed murmur as a cart eluded me: he shot out of his chair to summon the Watercress Lady. He offered me the first serving, then helped himself to a pile of the greens studded with cloves of garlic and downed them with absolute, beaming gusto. *Gusto:* that was the word I was thinking as I watched him chew and felt my stomach do a flip. John's appreciation of food was warm and sensual. He was curious, enthusiastic, and eager to try new things. All of this was obvious to me as I watched him happily bite the head off a whole shrimp.

Like most of the adults who had populated my childhood, John was cultured, articulate, and funny. But unlike anyone to whom I was related, John was a natural-born homemaker. He had a strongly developed domestic flair, and on our third date confessed to me that having a home and family was his greatest dream, and that he wanted to get married and have his first child by the time he was thirty years old.

"I don't want to freak you out," he explained nervously, "but if I'm going to get my heart broken, I want to know now, before things with us go any further."

"Oh, no," I said, "I'm not freaked out at all." Inside, my heart knew I had just won the jackpot. I was used to dating men who said things like "I don't want to be your boyfriend. I don't want to be anyone's boyfriend, okay?" To which I had learned to nod happily, saying things like "Oh God, me neither" in reply. John, from the very beginning, offered me a home, which is what I'd been looking for all along.

John loves to cook, and that's what he would do when I would visit him at his small, dark, roachy—and yet strangely cheery—apartment. (I guess it was John who provided the cheer—he had roaches living in his phone, for God's sake.) Interestingly, this was on the same block my parents lived on when they were in graduate school, and I like to think it is the block on which I was conceived.

Sitting at John's tiny kitchen table, throwing occasional longing glances at the cookie jar filled with Vienna sandwich cookies, I would eat peanuts from the shell and drink beer and chat with John as he popped a tray of chicken pieces into the oven to bake, then moved on to rice and black beans. The meals were delicious and simple, served with a greens-and-avocado salad that John, who had some European influences running through his own family, also preferred to eat as a second course.

John's kitchen bustle is cheerful, and I like being part of it. His cooking is a foundation of our relationship and a cornerstone of the home we proceeded to build together. He has ideas for dishes, he peruses cookbooks, he grinds his own dry rubs in our mortar and pestle. My regular contribution to our meals is salad and vinaigrette. They garner compliments, and when they don't, I fish for them. The salad habit is a positive one I've inherited from my mother, but the skills are my own. I learned to make vinaigrette from my friend Melissa, watching her cook in her parent's kitchen, and every Sunday morning at the farmers market I make sure we are well stocked with organic greens and herbs for the week. I am a harsh judge of tomatoes and choose them carefully. Cooking has become my novelty act, and these days it's mostly for our son, Clyde, who started on solids at six months.

I often seat Clyde in his high chair when I cook for him. I put one of his favorite CDs on the stereo and talk to him as I work, showing him the eggs in the bowl as I whisk them. My mother was a devoted intellectual guide, but when it came to the personal life of my family, she explained squat, leaving me to become a canny lip-reader and all-around psychic sleuth. In contrast, I like to let Clyde know exactly what's going on, even at mealtime. I announce his plate of food as it lands on his tray: "Clyde, for breakfast you're having a scrambled egg, a waffle, and hot buttered apples." As I bustle around my small, sunny kitchen and meticulously organized pantry, I find true joy, tweaking the arrangement of spice jars or sighing heavily as I return our majolica butter dish to its rightful spot, on the left-hand side of the dairy-centric top shelf of the fridge, next to the eggs.

Clyde's meals are consistent: breakfast is at eight, lunch at noon, dinner at six. He eats sitting down at the table, never wandering around, and there is no rampant snacking. We put thought into what we serve him. Nothing fancy, but no junk. Mostly, we want his meals to be tasty, appetizing, and nutritious. I do a lot of corn tortilla quesadillas, fruit salads, and fresh veggies, introducing new things (most recently, natural peanut-butter-and-jelly sandwiches, artfully constructed with no sog to speak of), which he is always open to trying. We also have fish sticks and Trader Joe's chicken nuggets in the freezer and thinly sliced deli counter turkey in the crisper—all-American "kid food" that long ago I fruitlessly begged my mother to buy. John cooks hearty staples like meat loaf, black bean soup, and red sauce. Two years old, Clyde has also been known to enjoy my quite delicious tuna salad on wheat bread, sliced diagonally, and he has once or twice been served noodles with butter and ketchup. The noodles weren't gummy, and the ketchup was only about a tablespoonful—sort of a guttersnipe's tomato paste—and I added a diced fresh organic tomato, a spoonful of whole-milk cottage cheese, and a pinch of fresh herbs.

As for me, I will always be a Marzipan Eater at heart. Marzipan is so Old World, so old-school, so charmingly pre-war. Like the rest of the sweets I now sparingly enjoy out in the open, I can appreciate marzipan in moderation. But when I'm tucking in to a plate of John's dark-golden roasted chicken, stuffed with herbs and a whole lemon, with a side of crisp roasted potatoes and steamed asparagus, I don't hold back. After ten years of practice, it's perfect. Roast chicken fills our house with a cozy smell. Each time I bite into the incredible, juicy, flavorful results, I feel not just like everything's going to be okay but like it actually is.

• KATHY EBEL'S TUNA SALAD •

For this recipe, I rely on interim forking to create a smooth consistency, measure ingredients by sight and taste, and combine them in the precise order listed below.

Serves 1

1 can (6 ounces) chunk white tuna
(or one of those cool new 7-ounce pouches)

1 tablespoon sweet pickle relish

Dijon mustard (optional)

Generous pinch mixed chopped fresh herbs,
or a few snips fresh dill, or a few chopped scallions

Mayonnaise, preferably Trader Joe's brand

Drain the tuna and fork it into a stainless steel bowl; separate vigorously with the fork until the texture is fine. Add the relish and fork through. Add the mustard, if desired, and fork through. Add the mixed fresh herbs, or dill, or scallions. Add the mayonnaise last, being careful not to add too much.

Serve in a scoop over greens, or as a sandwich, preferably on toasted wheat, sourdough, or rye bread.

TUNA FOR CLYDE

Mix finely flaked tuna with Trader Joe's mayonnaise or your mayonnaise of choice. Spread a small amount of tuna on thinly sliced white bread, remove crusts, and cut into quarters.

• KATHY EBEL'S SIGNATURE VINAIGRETTE •

As with the tuna salad, the secrets to this recipe are adding the ingredients to a (stainless steel) bowl in the order listed, whisking between each ingredient, and judging measurements by sight and taste. Thanks go to Melissa and Sue Painter for their contributions to the recipe.

Serves 4

Half of a lemon
Honey
Dijon mustard
Freshly ground salt and pepper
Balsamic vinegar
Fancy olive oil

Squeeze the lemon into a stainless steel bowl. Add the honey (equivalent to a "quick splotch" from a squeeze bottle) and whisk. Add mustard and whisk. Add salt and pepper, to taste, and whisk. Add enough balsamic vinegar so that the stream from the bottle hits the bottom of the bowl and bounces to the surface. Whisk. Add the olive oil in a thin stream, similarly allowing the oil to bounce to the bottom of the mixture in the bowl and rise to its surface. Whisk in the oil to emulsify the dressing. Serve over farmers market mesclun, baby arugula, or baby spinach.

Note: The traditional oil to vinegar/lemon juice ratio is 3:1.

SECRET RED ONION TRICK

Prepare the vinaigrette ahead of time and place in a small bowl. Thinly slice a small red onion and stir it into the vinaigrette with a fork. Cover with plastic wrap and leave the vinaigrette at room temperature for an hour or so before dressing greens. The onion will soften in texture and mellow in flavor in the dressing marinade. This is an especially nice dressing for a plain salad with grilled chicken or fish.

• NOODLES WITH COTTAGE CHEESE FOR CLYDE •

All measurements are approximations. These daily recipes are strictly cook-by-sight and are suited to being tweaked to taste.

Serves 1

1 large pat salted butter

Freshly ground salt

1 cup noodles, like penne, ziti, rigatoni, or farfalle,
freshly cooked, still warm

1 teaspoon Heinz ketchup

1 tomato, diced

½ cup fresh or frozen peas, cooked

½ cup whole-milk cottage cheese

1 teaspoon chopped fresh herbs

Add the butter and salt to noodles in the bowl in which the noodles will be served and stir. Add ketchup and tomato and stir. Add peas, cottage cheese, and herbs. Stir well and serve.

NANCY BUTCHER

Young-Adult Novelist

One of my ultimate favorite foods is *natto*. I buy packs and packs of *natto* at a time from the Japanese supermarket to mix with raw quail eggs and scallions and soy sauce, and maybe a little bit of hot Japanese mustard. *Natto* is fermented soybeans. It's dark brown in color and very, very sticky. It has a pungent smell that many people—both American and Japanese—find offensive, in the same way some people find especially pungent cheeses offensive. But I happen to love it, I think because I used to eat *natto* all the time when I was a little girl in Japan. My mother would mix *natto* the way I do now, and serve it on top of rice with shredded nori seaweed. I loved watching her crack the raw egg and the sound of her chopping scallions on the wooden cutting board.

In Japan, rice is *the* main staple; it goes with *natto* and everything else. *Gohan* is the Japanese word for cooked rice, and it also means "meal." Growing up, I had rice for breakfast, rice for lunch, rice for dinner. The thought of a bowl of white rice is the best thing on earth to me. Some people eat mashed potatoes for comfort, or macaroni and cheese, or buttered toast. I eat plain white rice. I love the rich, buttery smell of it as it is cooking; the plain, hot, simple taste of it. I love how it is a vehicle for other things: *natto, tarako* (codfish roe, served raw or roasted), *umeboshi* (pickled plums). When I was a girl, I used to eat all kinds of things with it: I used to eat rice with butter and soy sauce; I used to eat rice with a raw chicken egg and soy sauce; rice with pickles. And, of course, rice with *natto* on top. My mother used to pack *onigiri*—rice balls—for my lunches, which are shaped with something inside them, such as *umeboshi*, or bits of salmon, or *tarako*, and wrapped in seaweed.

Rice definitely does something for me emotionally, and I'm not sure it's entirely healthy. I've written about food issues and trying to lose weight. One of the things the experts say is that you should never eat because you're depressed, because that's when you tend to overeat. I usually follow this advice, but in my less-than-healthy moments I don't, and sometimes I even border on binge eating. But I think there's also a gray area, where eating is not necessarily healthy or unhealthy; it's normal and familiar and comforting to go for something that satisfies an urge or a hunger or a need. If I feel a little bit blue, I put raw rice and water in my rice cooker, turn it on, and then savor the sound as the steam begins and then the click when the rice is done. I have an old, dented Japanese rice cooker that I've had for twenty years, with a lid that gets gooey as the rice is cooking. My mother bought it for me when I was in college; she was appalled that I didn't have a rice cooker in my dorm room along with my hot plate and toaster oven. The smell and the taste of rice just take me back. Much more tangibly and powerfully than reading a Japanese poem or seeing a beautiful silk kimono, I smell rice cooking and suddenly I'm six years old and I'm happily eating a bowl of rice in my cozy bed.

I grew up with a mother who had very fundamental ideas about what you're supposed to eat, and how much you're supposed to eat. She was also hyperaware of feminine virtues. In Japanese culture, eating a lot is considered unfeminine. I had a complicated relationship with my mother around food. On the one hand, I think she wanted me to eat a lot of what she served because if I didn't, I would be insulting her abilities as a chef—an important attribute for a Japanese woman. On the other hand, she wanted me *not* to eat a lot, because Japanese girls and women are supposed to be modest, dainty, delicate eaters, like Victorian women. The men are allowed to just pick up a bowl of rice and shovel it into their mouths. Women cannot do that; they're supposed to keep one hand on their bowl to show restraint. God forbid they should show any eagerness or gluttony. My mother also discouraged me from eating because she thought I should be thinner than I was. As a girl, I wasn't supposed to eat much food, and I certainly wasn't supposed to enjoy it.

Ironically, Japanese love food. There are all kinds of incredible things in the Japanese diet that I try to get here in the States, or that I can't and that I think about all the time. I can't find certain Japanese fish and shellfish, some of which probably don't even have names in English. I also can't find *tsukushi*, or field horse-tails, which are weeds (for lack of a better word) that used to grow next to the railroad tracks near my house in Tokyo. They look like short, skinny, brown asparagus. My family would pick them in the spring and then cook them in sake and soy sauce and sugar. Then eat them on white rice, of course.

Japanese love feeding people, I think because generosity and hospitality are so important to the culture—you are always supposed to think of others before thinking of yourself. In the States, if you drop in on someone, you might get a cup of coffee or a drink. Or maybe not. In Japan, if you drop in on someone—and you should bring food if you do, like a box of pastries or rice crackers—you will get a full, proper tea with pastries, fruit, and little sandwiches, or even a proper meal. There are all kinds of elaborate rituals you are supposed to follow around eating and being fed—after a meal, to signal what a feast it was, or beforehand, to acknowledge the fact that someone's about to feed you. Before a meal, you say "*Ita-daki-masu,*" loosely translated as "I will now partake." The host says "*Dozo,*" or "Please go ahead." After a meal, you say "*Gochi-so-sama-deshita,*" or "That was truly a feast." You do this even if you're at home with the family, eating a simple meal of leftovers.

In Japanese culture, you keep your appetites to yourself, whether they are food appetites or sexual appetites or other appetites. When you eat a meal and compliment the chef, you do so in order to pay respects to the chef, not to reveal your personal pleasure at having eaten the meal. Whatever pleasure is involved in food has to do with *giving* pleasure to your guest as a chef, not *receiving* pleasure as the eater, especially if you're a woman.

My mother is Japanese and my father is American. When I was ten years old, my parents split up and my Japanese mother brought my brother and me to Akron, Ohio, where my father's parents lived. My father stayed in Japan, partly because of work, partly because he liked Japan better than the United States, for reasons having to do with politics and culture. He is an old-fashioned man, and he likes the fact that in Japan men come first, women second. My father was a difficult person for my mother to deal with in terms of food. He loved all things Japanese, but he did not love Japanese food except for simple, plain things like *tonkatsu* (breaded pork cutlet). He liked cooked meat and maybe some cooked fish and basic rice, but he wouldn't eat sushi, or anything that was highly spiced—anything with garlic or ginger or even onions. I always felt it was such a waste for him to be in Japan, with all that glorious food he didn't enjoy.

My father was rarely pleased by my mother's cooking, even though she bent over backward to satisfy him. He had a motto: "If it's bad, I'll say something. If I don't say anything, it means it's fine." My mother would cook American things like hamburgers and steaks and spaghetti (if you can call that American). Japanese don't eat ice cream, but she got a recipe for something called White House Ice Cream, which was vanilla ice cream with raw eggs in it. We didn't have an ice-cream maker, so she poured the mixture into a metal ice tray and stuck the whole thing in the freezer. The result was a bunch of vanilla-and-egg-flavored cubes. I'm sure my father had something unfavorable to say about that. However, he did like Chinese food. So my mother, who was already a very good cook, decided when I was six years old and my brother was four to enter a Chinese cooking school.

Chinese cooking school was a half-hour subway ride from our house. My mother schlepped my brother and me along with her on weeknights after school because there was no one else to take care of us. The room was a big kitchen/classroom in a plain institutional building in downtown Tokyo, with an island in the middle with sinks, stovetops, piles of woks, Chinese platters, and dishes and bowls and steamers.

My brother and I sat along one wall, on a bench that in my memory was up high so that we could look down on the action. We were the only kids there. We watched the whole time, patiently, for hours and hours and hours, because we were expected to be very good and quiet.

About a dozen women were taught by an older Chinese man. They cooked elaborate things like roast duck and noodle dishes and whole fishes. The emphasis seemed to be less on the cooking than on the presentation—the duck would be cut into slices and then arranged to look like a big, graceful, flying bird. Cucumbers and radishes and carrots would be arranged to look like blooming roses and other flowers. All sorts of foods would be arranged like peacocks, or heavenly bridges, or landscapes. My mother would take a fish and cut it up and rearrange it to look like an enormous goldfish with lily pads. It was amazing to me that food could be presented that way.

Sometimes someone would offer food to my brother and me to try. I liked the simpler Chinese dishes, like noodles and roasted meats. I was freaked out by dishes that involved complicated sauces with weird, lumpy ingredients in them. Japanese cuisine uses few sauces, and the ones that are used are simple and smooth, like *ponzu* sauce, which is basically a citrus-flavored soy sauce, or *tonkatsu* sauce, which is a sweet/savory sauce made of ketchup, sake, *mirin*, ginger, garlic, Worcestershire sauce, and sugar. I remember eating some sort of dish they had made in Chinese cooking class, and biting down on a piece of raw ginger, and thinking it was awful. Couldn't they have grated it and made it disappear? The whole carp also scared me with their huge, bulging eyes and fat lips. I thought of carp as dirty fish that lived on river garbage. I couldn't imagine eating them.

My mother would make at home some of the Chinese dishes she learned in class. She made something called *mapo-dofu*, which is stir-fried tofu and ground beef with a lot of ginger in it. I hated it back then; my brother and I used to take it out to the deck to eat it, then throw it into the bushes and have a great big laugh about it. I love it now. In fact, I love many of those lumpy mystery foods and sauces I disliked back then. My father, though, was never satisfied.

When we moved to Ohio, my mother tried really hard again to make American food. Once, for the Fourth of July, someone asked her to bring potato salad to an afternoon barbecue. She had no idea what potato salad was. So she made mashed potatoes and tossed them with mayonnaise, and everybody thought she was crazy. People always teased her about her efforts to be, or sound, or look American. In hindsight, I realize this was extremely patronizing. The potato salad incident was an example of that; people thought it was "so cute" that Mitsuko was trying to make an American potato salad and messed up. I was embarrassed, partly because I was thirteen years old and was embarrassed by everything, but partly because, secretly, I wished I had a white American mother who was "normal" and knew how to act like an American and cook American foods.

Once we moved to America, my brother and I just wanted to be American. We wanted to eat at McDonald's every day. My mother would make us lovely rice and noodles and fish and pickles, but we rejected them all; we just wanted hamburgers. I thought they were so strange at first—hot cooked meat between two pieces of white bread; there was nothing like that in Japan. But I grew to like them, especially with lots of ketchup. My mother would throw me birthday parties and make Japanese food. In the neighboring town of Cuyahoga Falls, there was an "Oriental" food store that had a small assortment of Asian ingredients, and my mother had relatives ship ingredients from Tokyo. There was some fresh fish available in regular grocery stores, although nothing like what she could get in Tokyo, so she adapted. She would make smelt tempura, because smelt was plentiful in the Midwest. My friends would come to our house and look at the tempura and the sushi and the noodles and the pickles and be like "What *is* that?" And so I banned it all. I said, "Mom, I want to be American," and she tried very hard to accommodate me. In Akron, we were the only Asian Americans for five hundred miles. It wasn't until college that I learned that it was glamorous and exotic to be Japanese, and I met other Asian Americans, and I rediscovered all the foods of my childhood.

I always wanted my mother to teach me how to cook, but she was very proprietary about the kitchen. I would go in and say, "Let me help you. What are you making? How do you make that?"

"Get out of my kitchen!"

I don't think she wanted to be overtaken by me anywhere. It was important for her to stay on top and not allow me to become an accomplished woman in the kitchen, or an accomplished woman in other ways. I had to discover everything on my own. When I was in college, I went into a cheese shop to get some Swiss cheese and the man ahead of me was ordering something called Jarlsberg. And I said, "What's Jarlsberg?" I tried a slice; it was so extraordinary, nothing like plain old Swiss cheese. This was an eye- and palate-opening experience for me. But even before that, I have a flashback to when I was about sixteen years old. I went to Savannah with my best friend, Julie, and her parents, and they took us to a nice restaurant. I looked at the menu—and remember, I'd been eating Big Macs for years—and I ordered duck à l'orange and asked the waiter to substitute a watercress salad for the regular salad. Where did that come from? I don't know, but I remember a momentary high from ordering a substitution and a sense of power from exercising a culinary choice. That was an early sign of what was to come.

My mother loves cooking, and I'm sure I inherited that from her to some degree. Even though it was a negative experience to be banned from the kitchen, I could see how much pride she took in cooking. My American grandparents were lovely people, but they ate bland stuff three meals a day: roast beef with no flavor, no garlic, no nothing, and mashed potatoes and overcooked beans. My grandmother made lots of white rice, but American rice doesn't taste the same as Japanese—it's not as rich. Also, my grandfather would put sugar and milk on his rice, which I found bizarre. I could have grown up with only that as an example, but instead I grew up with my mother, who, whatever her faults, always made incredible meals and tried hard to please people. After she divorced my father, she married a man who was fourteen years younger than she was, an ex-hippie who was a strict vegetarian. My mother went from being a major Japanese and Chinese chef to cooking tofu and lentils. But my brother and I demanded more from her, and she made us whatever we wanted.

She still does. When I go to visit her in Ohio, she's got ten dishes waiting on beautiful plates. She might have a Chinese fried noodle dish and another noodle dish in broth; teriyaki chicken with *sansho* (lemongrass) pepper on top; fried rice;

plain white rice with various pickles—cucumber, carrot, radish—she makes herself; steamed *shumai* dumplings and pan-fried *gyoza*; maybe a curry (a sweet Japanese-style curry, though, with pickled ginger on the side, not an Indian-style curry); and various salads, like fruit salad and green salad and even a potato salad. And of course, all sorts of sake, green tea, soda, chocolates, and cookies. My visits home are reminiscent of my childhood. I'm still never sure if whether to please her I should eat a lot, or if I should eat delicately, like a Japanese woman is supposed to.

I hardly ever cook for her. The few times I have, I've made sure that my husband, Jens, was with me because my mother feels comfortable complimenting a man. In fact, Japanese women are supposed to compliment men profusely. So if I make her something and Jens has helped me, she says, "Jens, this is so good! Where did you learn to cook? You must give me the recipe." But she stays quiet about me, which is okay. I long ago gave up the idea that we were going to have a food relationship based on mutual admiration, or that we'd cook together. She's a needy person, and when she's in the kitchen, she comes first. The conversations during a lot of her meals consist of her saying, "I don't mean to praise my own cooking, but isn't this good?"

And we all say, "Yes, it's amazing."

"No, but it's *really* good!"

It's a family joke.

I've developed my own culinary identity, which I would say is Japanese with a little bit of Italian and a little bit of French and a little bit of traditional American mixed in. There's a dish I eat at a Japanese cafeteria that is great fusion: Italian white wheat pasta tossed with a creamy *tarako* sauce, with slivers of *nori* on top. I make things like that at home. I use Japanese buckwheat soba noodles for a lot of things, tossing them with various sauces or cooked vegetables—sort of a buckwheat primavera treatment. I also like marinating meats and fishes with Asian ingredients—soy sauce and scallions and ginger and lemon rind, for example—throwing them on the grill, and serving them with non-Asian sides like roasted potatoes, pasta salad, steamed vegetables with herbs. Or serving meat loaf with Japanese white rice. My new comfort food is basmati rice with butter, orange juice, and a few threads of saffron steeped in water.

I get obsessed with and excited about ingredients. I love making whatever's fresh and seasonal. In the fall, I make my own version of vichyssoise with potatoes, leeks, beets, and crème fraîche. In the spring, I like to make pasta carbonara-style, with cream, lemon, and asparagus instead of bacon. When I go to the store or to the farmers market, I tend not to go with an idea in mind—*I must have this*. I go and I see something that looks really fresh and good, I buy it and I think about it all day, and then I go home and I cook. In the spring, my local farmers market has spinach (so sweet you can eat bags of it, raw, with nothing on it whatsoever), strawberries, asparagus, garlic greens. In the summer, I get tomatoes, amazing corn, melons, peppers, squashes, microgreens for salads, Chinese greens like pak choy for stir-fry, lettuces, potatoes (yellow, red, blue, fingerling), haricots verts, leeks, baby beets that come in different colors, including bright orange. In the fall, there's the sense of harvest—so much fresh food, so cheap and plentiful, everything must go!—with all the pumpkins and winter squashes. There's the lamb lady, who has extraordinary lamb as well as beautiful dyed yarns. One of my favorite stands, Paul Arnold's, had squash blossoms once: delicate and orange and lovely. I asked Mrs. Arnold how to prepare them. She said to dip them in egg yolk and white flour and fry them quickly in hot oil. Then eat them immediately with a bit of coarse salt. I did that—they were delicious.

I always buy way too much at the farmers market.

Another way I eat is exactly the opposite: I'll get a craving for something and my entire day will revolve around trying to satisfy that craving. I'll say to Jens, "I have to have a steak; if I do nothing else, I have to have a steak." And he'll spend the day planning a steak dinner to make for me. He'll plot out what kind of cut he should get; where we're going to get it; will we have a sauce with it or just a little salt and pepper and lemon juice, maybe a little garlic; what we're going to eat with it; what kind of red wine we should drink with it. And then the steak comes and it's the highlight of my day. I could have felt very mediocre about my first, now ex, husband, but on our first date we went to a movie, and afterward, we had to make a decision about whether we'd eat or not. Fairway supermarket was close by. He looked at the meat counter and said, "They have some very nice sausage; why don't I make some of that for you with tortellini?" And I was already there with a second date. Being fed is the ultimate luxury. When I'm fed, I feel nurtured, I feel mothered. I must have longed for that as a child—maybe it was the bit of comfort I had amid the discomfort, and food was the place where I found happiness. And I still do.

I remember when I was living alone in the city. I had no roommates, I had no relationships, and that's when I first noticed that I didn't like cooking for myself. There were times when I would literally make popcorn for dinner. This was due to loneliness and self-destructiveness, both. But it also had a positive spin; it was my version of a bachelor's existence, and there was a romantic, edgy feeling about it. When I was with my first husband, we always ate together except on Wednesday night, which was tennis night. He belonged to some old men's club and they'd play tennis and go out for a beer afterward. It would be my one night on my own. So I would get Kraft Macaroni & Cheese, and take a lot of onions, slice them up, put some olive oil on them and roast them. I'd make the entire box of macaroni and cheese, and I'd throw the roasted onions on top, and I would sit in front of the television. I just loved that. I loved being alone. I also loved the ritual of it: it was an indulgence I could count on every week. Maybe it had that comfort-food element to it and that was why it was so appealing, but to be honest, something disgusting can taste really good. Cool Ranch Doritos taste good, but if you read the ingredients, you'll never eat them again in your life.

There are a few things I'll make just for myself now, and when I do, I feel proud. It's as if I've allowed myself a break, or given myself a massage, and it feels better than when I eat just a carrot stick or a bowl of cereal. I have three paradigms. One is chickpea salad. I open up a can of chickpeas and I throw in some feta cheese and chopped scallion and tomato and cucumber, olive oil, and lemon juice, and it takes two and a half minutes to make. Another is soba noodles. I boil them, rinse them in cold water, and toss them with a little sesame oil, soy sauce, some rice wine vinegar, sesame seeds, and scallions, and whatever vegetables I have lying around. And the third thing is a salad of any kind. If I'm cooking vegetables the night before for dinner, or meat, I put a little extra aside to mix the next day with spinach or mesclun, hard-boiled egg, maybe some pecans, and a homemade vinaigrette. I manage to make one of these three things for lunch almost every day, and put it on a plate, and sit down to eat.

I don't know if not liking to cook for myself is an extension of the other ways in which any of us has a hard time taking care of ourselves. Every night, I give my eight-year-old son, Christopher, a bubble bath, and he loves it. But I don't know the last time I took a bath. I give him a bath and I think, "This is so simple and basic; he needs this—it cleans him and relaxes him before bedtime. Why don't I do this for myself?" The same is true about cooking. I was meeting my cowriter on a book, and my editor insisted that I meet him for lunch or drinks at a restaurant. I said, "No, I'm going to cook for him." And my editor said, "That's not professional, you've never met this guy and you're going to cook for him?" I said, "We're coming together on this book, I want him to like me and trust me, I'm going to cook him a meal." We argued about this for hours. And then the writer came over and I made beautiful lamb chops pan-roasted with lots of fresh tarragon, potatoes on the side, haricots verts, Australian Syrah, Manchego cheese from Spain. It was a lovely lunch. Cooking is a deep and obvious thing, except when it comes to doing it for myself.

These days, I like to cook with Jens. We share this great joy in talking about dinner and planning it, and pulling out cookbooks or improvising, and we'll go shopping together. When it actually comes to the cooking, we delegate. He'll be in charge of the meat or fish, if there's some animal involved—the "man's" job. I tend to make everything else: the side dishes and the salads and maybe a dessert. No matter what we're eating, I always set the table with a white tablecloth and linen napkins and Wedgwood china and real glasses. I'll put on a John Coltrane CD and light the candles. It's so much easier to enjoy the food, and appreciate each other's company, when we're not eating off plastic plates under bright lights with a sense of "Hurry up, scarf it down!"

Sometimes, I take Christopher out to Japanese restaurants. He orders a bowl of white rice and maybe some egg sushi. I get nori and put it on everything; I have sheets of it brought to the table and I rip it up and put it on my noodles and throw it on my rice. And Christopher has taken to doing that; he'll rip up nori and put it on whatever he's eating. I make a point of telling him about what I'm eating and why, and how I used to eat this as a little girl. I try to let him know how nice it is, these connections with food. I'm hoping he'll remember them as he's growing up. I want Christopher to remember candlelight and John Coltrane and the scene of Jens and me in the kitchen kissing and cooking and drinking wine. I don't have good memories of sitting at the table with my family, but I want him to.

• COLD BUCKWHEAT NOODLES •

Serves 4

1 package (8 ounces) buckwheat soba noodles
Memmi (see note)
Powdered *wasabi* (optional)
3 scallions, chopped fine, white and green parts
2 sheets nori, torn into small pieces

Boil buckwheat noodles as directed on the package.

While the noodles are cooking add 1 part *memmi* and 3 parts cold water to four very small bowls or cups (preferably the size of tea cups) and stir to mix. Adjust ratio to taste, if desired.

For the *wasabi*: in a small bowl, mix a small amount of *wasabi* with enough water to form a paste.

When the noodles are done, drain and run under cold water until they are chilled. (You can also achieve this effect by soaking the cooked noodles in a bowl of ice water, then draining.)

Put the cups of *memmi* on four separate dinner-size plates. Put the buckwheat noodles in equal portions on the plates. Sprinkle the noodles with chopped scallions and nori pieces. Serve the *wasabi* separately, on a small plate or in a small bowl.

To eat: mix a small amount of *wasabi* into the *memmi*, if desired. Dip the buckwheat noodles into the *memmi*, one bite at a time.

Note: Memmi is a soy-sauce-based soup base, available in Japanese grocery stores.

· NATTO ON RICE ·

Serves 4

1½ cups uncooked white rice

2 cups cold water

3 packages of prepackaged *natto* mix (see note)

Soy sauce

2 scallions, chopped very fine, white and green parts

1 sheet nori, torn into small pieces

4 raw quail eggs (optional)

Rinse rice in a colander until the water runs clear and cook in the water, either in a rice cooker or in a pan. This should take about 20 minutes. In the meantime, allow *natto* mix to come to room temperature. Mix it with the enclosed flavoring packages in a bowl. Add soy sauce to taste. Add most of the scallions to the *natto* mix, reserving a small amount for garnish.

Spoon the rice into bowls. Spoon the *natto* mixture on top in equal portions.

Sprinkle nori on top, along with the reserved scallions. If desired, break a quail egg on top of each bowl. The quail egg can be mixed in with the rice and *natto*, for extra flavor.

Note: Natto is available in Japanese grocery stores in the refrigerated section, in packs of three. Each packet is 50 grams (approximately 2 ounces).

PANKTI SEVAK

Biologist

I don't remember my mother cooking when I was a kid as much as I remember my aunt Divya cooking. Divya cooked because she lived with us and my mom worked, and Divya also took my sister and me to school and did all the chores. The interesting thing is that my aunt wasn't as good a cook as my mother. My mom loved to cook and eat, and she appreciated a good thing. My aunt cut corners, incorporating things like frozen vegetables. My mother, absolutely not. She had a garden and whatever came out of the garden she'd cook—eggplant, green beans, spinach, cucumbers, four kinds of tomatoes. She loved tomatoes, even though they don't really have tomatoes in India. Whatever she cooked, it was always fresh, and it was always made by hand.

When my mother came to the kitchen, she would make snacky things like *poha*, which is pounded rice with potato and chili. And *kitcheree*, which is rice and dal put in a pressure cooker and cooked so it comes out like porridge. You can spice it however you want. On good days, when my mother had the luxury of time, we would have it with a few garlic cloves and yogurt. Or she might put vegetables in it, and spices like turmeric and asafoetida and pepper. *Kitcheree* is comfort food, and it's a whole food—a complete meal; it's my dad's favorite thing in the whole world. He likes to eat it with overcooked spinach.

Puris are puffed breads; my mom loved these, and also spiced rolled breads, and elephant ears. Elephant ears are huge leaves; to prepare them, you make a very spicy paste out of *besan*, which is chickpea flour, and you paint the leaves with it, roll them like rugelach, and then cut and steam them. The leaves have a mild, bitter flavor, and the paste is sweet and spicy and savory. They're out of this world. If you really want to go crazy for a party, you can fry them after you've steamed them so they get crunchy.

My family is from the Gujarat region of India, and Gujarati food is all vegetarian. My experience of it is that it's simple, even though a typical Gujarati meal has at least three or four different things in it. A meal is pretty much always eaten on a *thali*, which is either a segmented metal plate or a flat plate that holds several small bowls. It always includes pickles and condiments. Pickle you make only once a year, when it's mango season, say. But condiments you can make at any time, and my family will make them out of anything. My stepmother makes pickled carrots with mustard seed and lemon juice. My grandmother takes the end of the cauliflower she's not going to cook and chops it into small pieces and makes a pickle out of that. I was raised in a family where you eat everything on your plate and you get every grain of rice out of the bowl. You waste nothing.

In a Gujarati meal, there's usually a bread, always dal and rice, and a vegetable. Gujaratis eat their dal on the thin side, like soup. Gujarati cooking uses things like fresh green chili, and since Gujarat has a lot of farmland, there are many fresh ingredients available. A lot of Gujarati cooks put sugar in their food—everything they make has a sweet aftertaste to it; that's how Divya cooks. But I prefer Indian food to be savory and spicy. So did my mom, and so does my grandmother.

A lot of my memories of cooking are from my grandmother's house in India, because I spent many summers there. My grandmother's house has thirty people living in it. The women are always hanging out in the kitchen, talking, praying, singing, and cooking together. When they cook, first they chop all the vegetables—remember, they're chopping vegetables for thirty people so this is a big job. Then they make chapatis for thirty people: then they make dal for thirty people; they cook on the floor with a stove attached to a gas tank, because they don't have counter space. There's a whole division of labor with a rotating duty, with four or five people in the kitchen together. You don't cook alone for thirty people; you cook with three other women, and they're all in charge. My grandmother cooks with her daughters-in-law, of which there are three, and with her sisters-in-law, of which there are three. They change roles every day in a very organized and systematic way. The women talk as they cook, but it's strangely meditative at the same time because of the singing.

Cooking is about duty—that's just the way we do things in my family. And it's very communal. I remember we would spend a day when the dals were delivered, sifting through them. All the women would be out on the patio with big plates, and we'd go through the dals and take all the rocks out of them to make sure they were good to cook with. This chore, and everything related to cooking in my grandmother's house, was very predictable, but it wasn't routine in a dysfunctional way. I could always find someone in the kitchen doing this, that, or the other thing, and I knew exactly where I could seamlessly fit in and help.

When I was very young, every two or three years my grandmother was with us in America for six months at a time. My mother died when I was thirteen years old, and then my grandmother came to live with us for a few years. She was a huge part of my life. I would come home from school and she'd say, "This is what I did today!" And she'd have some hot afternoon snack that she'd made just for me. The things she cooks well she cooks to complete perfection. For example, every single one of her chapatis lines up exactly on top of the other. In India, to serve thirty people, there would be a stack of a hundred chapatis, each one exactly the same. It was so satisfying to see that. My grandmother would make things like *jelabi* sweets and *puran puri,* a bread that's stuffed with a sweet milk fudge and nuts and raisins—complicated things that no one bothers to make. It was exciting for her that I would come home at three P.M. and we would eat something together.

Sometimes in America, she tried new things; she got joy from that. Maybe she'd find new ingredients—she might use different kinds of milk products, for example. A lot of it was learning to use the microwave. She never made whole dishes in it, only peripheral stuff to help cut down on preparation time. She wasn't microwave dependent at all, but she found it made a few things much easier, like *khandvi,* which is a soft, lemony crêpe made from chickpea flour. Normally you have to stand over the stove for an hour to make it, stirring out the lumps, but you can make it in the microwave in fifteen minutes and stir it three times and it's perfect. This was a compromise, my grandmother knew, but it didn't make the *khandvi* weird at all.

My grandmother went out of her way to make things I liked; this was one of the major ways I felt taken care of by her. Having to feed myself as an adult, on some days I can't get over it. Food for me is about family and sharing. My grandmother would ask me, "What do you want to eat this week?" or, "Do you want me to make this?" It wasn't about a special occasion, it was about "This is the way I bring joy to other people." The boys in her house work in an office, and even now, at the age of eighty, she'll decide in the middle of the day that she's going to make *poha* and have the *pune* (courier) come and take it to them when they would be getting ready to have a snack, as a surprise, in a tiffin lunchbox. And it's not just the *poha;* she'll send chutney along with it, and a thermos of tea. Cooking is a way she shows her love for people. And she's a damn good cook and she knows it, and she gets to eat it, too.

My family in India are Brahmins—temple keepers—and they offer food to the gods every day. There's a little shrine in my grandmother's house, and in the morning, my family opens the temple and dresses the little deities who live inside it, and strings them with garlands—my grandmother makes them garlands and also clothes and jewelry. And then they sing to them, full-on, with the tabla. When I visited, I would always wake up to singing at seven in the morning. Then the deities get a bath, and then a plate of fruit, and then a meal. A little bit of everything that's been prepared for the family's breakfast is put on a silver *thali* and taken down to the shrine; it's brought back up a few minutes later and mixed in with the rest of the food.

Since my family worships Krishna, and Krishna loves sweets, every day there is also a sweet offering. That's another thing my grandmother is amazing at—making sweets by hand. To this day, I'm a total snob about sweets, because I grew up on my grandmother's; I never ate them out of a shop. Since she made them as an offering, they were always small and special, bite-size, versus when you go to a shop, where the sweets are huge. I always wonder, How am I going to eat that? Food in India, at least in my family, is seen as holy. It's a symbol of nourishment and strength and life. That's part of why my grandmother has the attitude that you should eat fresh food; it's giving you health.

At mealtime in India, we would always sit down to eat at two large square tables, and fifteen people ate at the same time. Usually the men would be at one table, and the kids would be at the other, and there would be a plate in the middle of each table with at least four kinds of pickle on it, and chutneys, salt, lemon, whatever vegetable condiments had been made that day, and a bowl of yogurt. There would be a table in between where all the bowls of food sat, and one woman would stand there and serve. The rest of the women would be in the kitchen doing other things, and they would eat together, after. Whoever was in the middle would serve us and watch our plates, and as we were finishing something she'd give us some more of it. It was very interactive. You'd talk about your day and make fun of each other across the table.

It was always hard to come back to the States because it felt lonely, as though there were a lack of people. Meals were boring then. But when my grandmother came to stay, meals had the same aspect to them that they did in India. She would always make hot chapatis while we were eating. She'd feed us, keeping an eye on my sister, my dad, and me, and whoever else was there. And then I would make chapatis for her, and I would sit with her while she had dinner so she didn't eat alone. This has always been a rule in our house: you never eat alone.

I got home from school pretty early, and I would gravitate toward the kitchen. I always belonged there; it always felt safe. I liked not having to talk, and I could do repetitive things. I liked the product that came out of it. And I still do. I love to chop vegetables—it makes me so happy. I could chop and I could be in the company of other people without having to talk or explain myself, and be accepted for who I was. I always felt weird around other children, but I never felt weird around old ladies. There were things I understood about the way the world worked that kids didn't. After my mom died, it was hard to be around teenagers. But I liked being around women because I felt they wouldn't hurt me. Being around kids, I felt teased, I felt judged, I felt they didn't want to play fair, and that hurt my feelings because I was very sensitive. I never felt that way in the kitchen. You have to make the meal; it has to get done. There's no room to mess around. Everybody has their own personal space and their own task; you do your thing and I do mine. Then you sit down to eat, and you appreciate your own skill and the skill of the other cooks.

I did my homework in the kitchen while my grandmother was cooking, and I talked to her at the same time. We hung out till we went to sleep, and we would also sleep in the same bed; we spent a lot of time together. I learned a lot from her, about pacing yourself, and that you should always make enough food for leftovers. I learned to be efficient with food: not to make a million dishes but to make three things simply, and not to be afraid of fire. I learned that making food is about sharing it with other people. What's always been painful for me about my stepmother is that she's bizarrely greedy in the kitchen. She makes things the way she likes them, and she doesn't see what's happening around her. She doesn't do this to hurt me, but it inspires the worst kind of pain. For a few years after my grandmother returned to India for good, I could barely sit at my stepmother's table and eat with her, because it was where I felt the most lonely.

I've been going to an ashram in upstate New York since 1996, and I've been cooking on and off there since 1997. It is a retreat site, a place for renewal and reflection. When I began cooking at the ashram, I worked with a man who had been cooking there for twenty years or so, who talked to me about food the way my grandmother used to. He would say that food was holy; that it should be served with love and cooked with love, or good energy; that when you use fresh ingredients, food has life and offers sustenance. I learned all over again how to sit, eat, and taste food with awareness. This made eating more sensual and enjoyable, but also made me feel like I could choose good things for myself to eat, with consciousness. It has also reminded me how strongly I feel about not wasting, and about taking only what you need or know you will be able to finish. We Americans are so gross and greedy sometimes, so unaware and super-sized.

I learned to cook very large meals at the ashram, and now I regularly prepare full meals there for a hundred people or more. I love to make Indian food for that many people. Before, when I thought of large quantities of Indian food, I thought of those greasy Indian buffets where everything tastes the same. That doesn't happen with food at the ashram; it maintains its integrity and freshness. I've learned a lot about combining flavors but still keeping them simple so that the life of the food can come through. Ultimately, I've come to think of food as something of the earth, something that should be simple and clean.

I also learned to bake at the ashram, and that taught me patience, discipline, attention to detail, and how to follow recipes, as I had rarely cooked from a recipe before I learned to bake. I've learned lots of lessons in the ashram kitchen that have been important to me in my daily life. Cooking and baking are processes that allow me to get lost for a little while, and to reflect and create. Always before I begin cooking at the ashram, and then when the food is done, I offer up what I have made. The act of praying over the food keeps me humble.

In my own kitchen, I have only one knife and a handful of pans, and I can make myself a meal with just a few things. I went to a friend's house for dinner the other night, and she had a lot of things, which I think is cool—I would love to have appliances, but I don't have the space for them and, really, I just don't need them. My friend had this fancy cheese grater and she asked me, "Do you have one of these? Why not?" And I said, "I'm too utilitarian to own one of those. I just take out a hunk of cheese and grate it onto my pasta." It's not better or worse, it's just the way I do it.

I like shopping for food. There are days when I'm exhausted and I can't think about it. When that happens, it happens, but I'm always happy to get back into the kitchen. I like coming home at the end of the day and pouring a glass of wine and making whatever it is I'm going to make. What's sad about it is that I don't have someone to share it with. But the act of cooking is great. First of all, it's less expensive than eating out, and I love saving money—I'm cheap. Second, I can pretty much make anything I can get out, better, and that gives me a strange sense of satisfaction. Cooking for me is never more complicated than going to the market before I get home and picking out something like a piece of tofu, then taking it home and tossing it in the pan. How hard is that?

My typical meal consists of greens—I buy three kinds of greens at the market for the week—and rice that I throw in the pressure cooker, or a sweet potato that I throw in the oven. I cook my tofu in a pan, take it out, and put it in the toaster oven to keep warm, and then I cook the greens: there's my dinner in one pan. I like the efficiency of that, and it takes twenty minutes. I would spend the same amount of time waiting for something to show up at my doorstep that I wouldn't like as much.

My sister likes everything she eats to have sauce and a lot of flavor. I could make a meal with plain squash and spinach and be happy. A lot of people like their food to be very flavored, but I like to taste the food that I'm eating. I don't need to do much to it aside from warm it up; it just varies how I warm it up. My new thing is putting pecans in with my Brussels sprouts, because I happen to have some in my freezer. But once they're gone, I'm probably not going to go out and buy more. It's true that I like Indian food to be spiced, but I don't have to eat that way every day. My palate is more evolved than that. I'm willing to try things and like them for what they are rather than trying to make them taste like what I'm accustomed to.

When my sister and I cook together, we'll usually do it her way, in her kitchen. I'm pretty good at deferring to her, because I don't *dislike* for food to be savory with sauce; it's just that I like it to be plain, too. Sometimes she likes to learn things from me so she'll ask me to show her. Sometimes we'll do a combination of things—two things that go well together—and she'll do one and I'll do the other and we'll both have our way.

But I'm happy to cook alone. I don't need the help.

I have a scientific approach to most things. I'm systematic, and I think it's important to know certain principles—in the lab, or in the kitchen—in order to work through a problem. In cooking, you have to know what good ingredients are, how to chop well, what the basic flavors of ingredients are so you can learn how to combine them. When you know the basics, then you can adapt. There's an underlying discipline in science—and in cooking, as in any art.

• KITCHEREE •

Any kind of dal can be used for this recipe, but I like and almost always use split mung beans. The ratio of dal to rice can be altered depending on how thick you like your kitcheree. My sister, Purvi, uses one-third cup rice to two-thirds cup dal.

Serves 4

1 cup basmati rice, well rinsed

1 cup dal, rinsed

1 teaspoon grated ginger, or to taste

Salt, to taste

¼ to ½ teaspoon turmeric

Pinch of *hing* (asafoetida) (see note)

5 cups water

2 teaspoons ghee (clarified butter) (see note)

½ teaspoon whole cumin seed

1 to 2 dried red chilies (optional)

6 to 8 curry leaves (see note)

In a medium saucepan, combine the rice, dal, ginger, salt, turmeric, *hing,* and water. Bring to a boil over high heat, then turn down to medium heat and cook slowly for about 30 minutes. Add more water as the *kitcheree* cooks if you like it to be softer; I prefer my *kitcheree* to have a porridge-like consistency.

In a separate saucepan, heat *ghee* over medium-high heat. When it's hot, add whole cumin seeds and fry until they pop; add chilies if desired and fry until they blister. Then add curry leaves and fry until they bloom, 10 to 15 seconds. Add this mixture immediately to the cooked rice mixture and stir well to combine.

Serve with yogurt, pickle, or pickled onions. To make pickled onions: Julienne an onion and mix with lemon juice and salt to taste; allow to sit for 30 minutes before serving.

Note: Hing (asafoetida) is a pungent resin that is sold in powder form in Indian grocery stores.
Note: Ghee is available in Indian markets, or make your own by melting butter over a low flame and then straining out the milk solids.
Note: Curry leaves are the leaves of the Murraya Koenigii plant, readily available in the produce section of many Indian markets. They can be frozen for a month or two to maintain their freshness.

• ELEPHANT EARS (ARVI-NA-PATRA) •

Serves 6 to 8

15 to 20 elephant ear (*colocasia*) leaves

1 tablespoon jaggery (see note)

2 tablespoons hot water

2 cups *besan* (chickpea or gram) flour

2 teaspoons cayenne pepper, or to taste
(I like it spicy)

1 teaspoon turmeric, or to taste

1 teaspoon salt, or to taste

Juice of half a lemon, or to taste

2 teaspoons vegetable oil

½ teaspoon mustard seeds

½ teaspoon sesame seeds

6 to 8 curry leaves (see note, p. 42)

Shredded coconut and cilantro for garnish

Wash the leaves and slice away their thick stems. Dissolve jaggery in 2 table-spoons of water and add to the flour, stirring well. Add the cayenne, turmeric, salt, and lemon juice to the flour and mix, then add just enough water so that the mixture forms a paste that can be spread onto the leaves without running off—about the consistency of pancake batter. The paste should taste strongly tart and sweet, as ultimately the flavor will be diluted by the leaves; adjust spices accordingly.

Lay one leaf flat on a dry countertop. Spread paste onto the leaf; don't over-coat, but be sure to cover the entire surface. Place another leaf on top of the first one. Spread with more paste. Roll the two leaves together tightly, like sushi rolls. Set aside. Continue in this way until all the leaves are used up.

Bring water to a boil in the bottom portion of a steamer. Place the rolls in the top portion of the steamer and cover. Steam for about 20 minutes, until the dough is no longer sticky.

Cut the leaves into 1-inch slices. Set aside.

Add vegetable oil to a pan over medium-high heat. Add mustard seeds and fry until they pop. Add sesame seeds and fry until they brown slightly. Add curry leaves and fry until crisp. Add the sliced elephant ears to the pan and cook until they crisp a little, turning once with tongs. Remove to a platter and garnish with shredded coconut and cilantro.

Note: Jaggery is unrefined lump sugar that has a very particular, earthy flavor. It can be found in Indian grocery stores. Equal parts white and light brown sugar can be used as a substitute.

MAYA KAIMAL
South Indian Cookbook Author

My maternal grandparents were from Boston, and I feel deeply rooted in that city. During my childhood, every Sunday we drove to my grandparents' house in Winchester, Massachusetts, for supper. During the Depression, my grandfather had in the backyard there what he called a victory garden, that World War II phenomenon—everyone with their own small plot, growing what they could. He grew tomatoes and corn and lettuce and strawberries and green beans. My grandmother, who was a very economical home cook, canned all her own fruits and vegetables, including some my grandfather grew. I particularly remember eating her bread-and-butter pickles, which she put out at every summer event.

My grandparents built their house when they got married, right before the Depression. It was a modest Dutch Colonial two-story three-bedroom house. It had hardwood floors and gumwood trimming, a little one-car garage and a screened-in porch and a fireplace. The house smelled like grandparents, like fabric that has been around for a long time, and cedar chests. My grandmother's drapes covered the windows—she sewed all the curtains and knitted the blankets—and her framed needlepoint hung on the walls. The house had one of those chime clocks that would ring every quarter hour. Spending the night and hearing one ding on the quarter hour and two dings on the half hour was such a powerful sensation; it was *so* my grandparents, and it was so American.

The scent of my grandparents' house was completely different from ours, and I attribute it all to the cooking. Nana cooked good, solid New England food. She made cod with salt pork, potatoes, and onions, and roast beef hash with poached eggs and ketchup. She made baked beans with brown bread, and corn chowder, and fried chicken, and fish with tartar sauce. My father really liked her cooking, even though it was nothing like his; everything in our house got spiced because of his taste. But he respected that my grandmother was a very able cook. And we all enjoyed the weekly ritual of driving to Nana and Grandpa's house for Sunday supper. My mother remembers dinners in that same house growing up as being utterly silent, but that's not what it was like when I was growing up and the five of us came over to eat.

Nana was good at making sweets, like chocolate cake, brownies, and soft raisin cookies called "hermits." She was a tiny little lady who loved to say, "I can eat all the chocolate I want and never gain an ounce." She had an incredible sweet tooth and always kept chocolate in the top drawer of her buffet. My brother and I could hardly get through dinner, thinking about what was in that drawer. Nana also had a real knack for making fudge. Only she could make it—it was really her thing, her specialty—and it was dense and creamy. It's a little tricky making fudge. Maybe you have to know the nuances of making it; you do it so many times it becomes a pleasant ritual and a point of pride. When it's not your ritual it feels like a task, and neither my mother, my siblings, nor I have mastered Nana's fudge technique. It's not our specialty, it was Nana's, and it's one of those things that passed with her.

I loved spending the night over at Nana's house because of the food she made that we never had at home. We'd always get a root beer float after dinner, when we were in our pajamas. I loved the special glasses Nana used that were, in my mind, designed for root beer floats. I think they were really café au lait cups; they were curved and kind of tapered like shrunken Coke glasses, and they sat in little brass holders that had handles on them. The idea of having just the right vessel to complete the experience is something I inherited from Nana. But I see my aunts and cousins in India conferring about the same thing.

And for the most part, when I'm thinking about presenting food, I'm thinking about Indian food. I need to have the right dish to contain the gravy and the right sort of spoon to be able to get a mixture of the liquid and the solid together. When I'm shopping for bowls, I'm thinking about different dishes I make. For *raita*, I use something I found in an antique store in Minneapolis. It's a beautiful, unglazed-exterior bowl with a glossy, deep-emerald-green interior, and it begged to have yogurt-and-cucumber *raita* in it. For rice, I have an angle-sided, shiny black lacquer-y looking bowl with a small pedestal base. To me, that says rice, and so rice goes in it. And I have a light celadon bowl of fine yet rustic porcelain that's the perfect middle size for my Indian stir-fried vegetables; it holds exactly the right amount for four people. Presentation is as important to me as the preparation. It's like clothes for food, what you bring the food out to the world in. When I'm making a meal, I'm also thinking about what vessels it will go in, and how the table will look.

Presentation is functional and it's aesthetic and it brings together all the things I'm already thinking about when I'm cooking. It gives me such pleasure to use these vessels and match them up in a particular way. People know this about me, so I get a lot of bowls as gifts. Every time we have people over for dinner, because we don't have a dishwasher, my husband asks me, "Can we please put out the pots with the food in them?" I throw my arms up: "No! No! I've got all these beautiful bowls that I've been collecting for a lifetime and I'm using them!" Nana had the same kind of love of bowls, as well as her own system of stacking them in her cupboard. She was the only one who knew exactly how they could stack, and when we'd be over and washing dishes, we could never get them in the right order. It had all been worked out, couldn't be improved upon.

Another vivid memory I have of sleeping over at Nana's was the smell of her great breakfast wafting up the stairs at six A.M. First the smell of coffee, then bacon would drift past my bed. Nana would take English muffins and cook them on a griddle instead of in a toaster, and she had a way of buttering and pressing them so they were smashed flat and crusty. I loved waking up in the early morning glow of Nana's bedroom, underneath the chenille bedspread, with that combination of smells that was so distinctly *her house*.

She had such a clear sense of how she wanted to do things. She was a bit of a perfectionist, I think; she had been a seamstress, and everything she did, from sewing to cooking, she was so precise about. The idea that she had this pride and love in putting together a meal really appealed to me. Affection was part of the process of cooking; it was built in. This must have been a pretty strong sensation for my mother, too, because when she went to college she majored in home economics.

But while Nana always cooked real New England food, if I were to try to define my mother's style of cooking, I would say it's eclectic and curious. Curious is how she is about the world, and interested in other places and people. We had a Japanese exchange student for a while, so she learned how to make sukiyaki and sushi. It wasn't what my friends were eating in Boston in the early '70s. They'd come over to play and say, "What's that? Smells good." There's also a sort of fearlessness that comes along with that curiosity. When my mother met my father, she was cooking pork chops and salad. Although he didn't yet cook at the time, my father had some ideas about how he liked his food, and he said, "In India, we cook our meat in liquid." She said that concept hit her like a thunderbolt. Her views on cooking totally changed at that point, and she started to move away from traditional American concepts of braising and frying and broiling. With that message or request from my father, she broadened her scope and looked around for other ways of doing things. She already had a good grounding in the mechanics of cooking from her home economics background. So when she visited India in 1961, four years after marrying my father, she could watch my father's mother cook in the kitchen and take notes and get it.

My mother's cooking evolved over the years, largely because of my father's interest in food that was spiced, or food that had complexity to it. It didn't have to be Indian, but it had to have some kick. Dad's classic comment at the table was: "Hmmm, needs more cayenne," no matter what he was eating. He was always jumping up and getting the Tabasco sauce or some version of chili. Indian men especially like to have their little dish of sliced green chilies on the side to take bites from, just to make their meal a little peppier. My mother's cooking came to incorporate his sensibility: "Let's make it a little zesty, let's throw some green chilies into that omelet."

On the weekends when I was growing up, my father would often make an Indian dinner. It was always very popular among our friends when he did. He is a physicist, and so he's very precise when it comes to measuring and methodology. He likes to know that there's a particular system for making something, and that it can be repeated. He's not interested in the mystery: why get it right once and never be able to repeat it? Every time he'd cook, he'd take careful notes on what he was doing. For many people, that's anathema. But what he was doing was building some frameworks, some systems, some patterns, finding ways of deconstructing Indian food: "A five-to-one coriander-to-cumin ratio really works with meat, but for vegetables, use four parts cumin to one part turmeric." That's how his mind works. It all makes sense, and there's a great dinner at the end.

When I was in college and wanted to make dinner for my friends, I wanted to make Indian food. By this point, my father had compiled a whole bunch of his best family recipes because he had started teaching an Indian cooking class. He sent them to me. I wanted to get the school to pay for the ingredients because we were all on the meal plan, and I thought, "They're already ordering the raw materials, so I should be able to use them to feed people." I found out I had to form an organization. Some of my friends were Indian and the food was going to be Indian, so I called it the Young Indians of Claremont Colleges—the YICCs. I used the tiny kitchenette in my dorm to cook; it was a place for making popcorn, basically. I borrowed the pots and pans from the kitchen. We used a little gathering room and showed some slides from my friend's trip to India and watched a Hindi movie.

I did all the cooking myself. It was not a bad first attempt, and the reason was that my father's recipes were so precise. The things that had driven him into cooking were nostalgia and science. He wanted to re-create the tastes he had grown up on. He had a sense of what the dishes should be like—how thick the gravy should be, what the spice mixture should taste like, what the predominant flavors should be—and used his very organized mind to figure out how to do it. It's such a pleasure to make this kind of food for people, and friends have come to expect that when they come to our house for dinner that they'll get a homemade Indian meal. It also gives me the opportunity to teach a little bit. With Indian cooking, it's crucial that you take each ingredient to a certain stage before moving on to the next one: the mustard seeds need to pop and turn gray before you add the dried red chili. And the dried red chili needs to blister and brown before you add the curry leaves. And the curry leaves need to sizzle and crisp before you add the ground spices. It's definitely not like making a stew, where everything gets tossed in together. You have to be patient to cook this way or else the flavors won't blend properly.

My husband loves it when I make *appam*, South Indian fermented rice pancakes. The batter is a little bit sweet from coconut and makes these lacy, puffy pancakes with crisp edges, like nothing anyone's ever had. I serve them with a thin, coconut milk–based curry, usually a vegetable curry like one of my aunties makes, flavored with ginger and green chili, and curry leaf, which is a predominant flavor in South Indian cooking. These are flavor combinations unique to the Kerala region of India, where dishes are carefully spiced—complicated in their seasoning, but balanced.

My mother and father cooked together quite a lot when they had those weekend dinner parties back in the '70s. It was constantly: "Chandran, that heat's too high."

"No it's not."

"Yes it is. You're going to burn that." My father likes to use really high heat, and he cooks in a zone—you can't talk to him; he's very focused on what he's doing. I love cooking with both of them. My mother is confident and relaxed in the kitchen. She knows exactly where she's going and what she's doing at every moment. She knows where everything is kept; she never has to go looking for things. My father has to hunt for the potato peeler for ten minutes. We've worked out this great dynamic with the three of us cooking in the kitchen when I visit. They let me be the chef. My mother is the sous chef and prep cook, readying all the ingredients. She has no ego in this at all: "What can I do to help? Can I chop the chicken? Dice the onions? Mince the ginger?" My father mixes the spices and steps in as the taster, the expert palate. He and I consult: Does it have enough salt? Does it need more lemon, or chili? We have sort of a conference about that, or I say, "What do you think, Dad, should I brown these onions more?" We all enjoy working with recipes and writing recipes—it must have something to do with the way we process information—so it makes sense that I wound up writing cookbooks.

The food my father made was clearly the thing that set our family's cooking apart from that of everyone else I knew—except, of course, our Indian friends. It was one of the ways I saw myself having a foot in two worlds. Each half enhanced the other, maybe partly because of the way my mother embraced the Indian-ness of my father. My mother liked going to India, she liked Indian food, she liked Indian art; before every trip she would plot out the museums and the monuments she wanted to see. There was a period when she wore saris to dress up, and every day, she wore my Indian grandmother's gold bangles. I saw my Indian side as a positive thing. Was there a distinction between the Indian and the American? Yes, but it made sense in the context of our lives and the way these two cultures existed together. Food is so much a part of my aunties' lives in India; like my mother, it's what they spend their day thinking about. Our lives are different in many, many ways, and some of that was hard to communicate or to get past when I would visit, but when it came to food, we easily connected. They saw that I really embraced my Indian half, and that I cared about these details of their lives, and that I felt the things they were doing were important.

Having a foot in two worlds was empowering; it allowed me to grow up with American values that were enriched by an Indian sense of family. When you're part of an Indian family, you're part of a very large, supportive network. I felt the comfort and benefit of being able to go to India and have so many people love me and want to know me and know what my life was like, and who would help me in any way they could. In researching my cookbooks, I talked to every family member about how and what they cooked. I came to understand how much Indian ideas about family and food have shaped me and enhanced the lessons I learned from my mother and her mother. I hope to be able to show my own children the rich ways that food connects us all.

• HODGE PODGE •

My mother was fond of this salty New England classic while growing up in Boston. It's a sturdy blend of salt cod, salt pork, potatoes, and onions that my grandmother learned from her in-laws. She made it for us when I was young, and, despite its monochromatic appearance, I loved the salty flavors contrasted by sweet onions and doughy dumplings, which she adapted from a recipe in an old edition of Joy of Cooking.

Serves 6

¼ pound dried salt pork, cut small

¼ pound bacon, cut small

6 or 7 good-sized onions, chopped

1 pound boneless salted codfish (not flaked) (see note)

6 or 7 medium potatoes, halved

Dumplings (recipe follows)

Pepper, to taste

In a large frying pan, fry the salt pork and bacon over medium heat until soft but not brown. Add onions, and cook until soft and slightly browned. Remove from heat and set aside.

While the onions are cooking, boil codfish until tender; drain and set aside. Boil potatoes until half done, then add dumplings to the pot, cover, and cook until done, about 20 minutes.

On a large platter, place potatoes in center and dumplings surrounding. Top with fish. Pour the onion mixture over this. Sprinkle with pepper.

Note: To soak salted codfish, rinse well in cold water, then place in a large bowl and cover with cold water. Let stand for one day, unrefrigerated, changing the water three times. Drain.

· DUMPLINGS ·

My mother never liked dumplings, so we have no family recipe of our own. These are adapted from The Fannie Farmer Cookbook, *twelfth edition, 1986, revised by Marion Cunningham, and are similar to the ones my grandmother made.*

2 cups flour

3 teaspoons baking powder

1 teaspoon salt

4 tablespoons shortening

¾ to 1 cup milk

Combine flour, baking powder, and salt in a bowl and stir to mix. Cut in shortening until mixture resembles coarse meal. Add ¾ cup milk and stir briefly with a fork. Add only enough of remaining ¼ cup milk to make the dough hold together. Drop spoonfuls of the dough into water with potatoes in Hodge Podge.

· FUDGE ·

My mother's mother was crazy about candy, though you'd never guess if from her 110-pound frame. She tasted See's Candy for the first time while visiting California in 1958 and came home with this recipe, though no one knows how she got it. All we knew was that she became an expert fudge maker, and to our delight she would often bring over a brick of this creamy confection.

1 large can (1⅔ cups) evaporated milk

4½ cups sugar

3 cups chocolate chips

2 cups nuts, coarsely chopped

1 pound margarine or butter, melted,
plus more for oiling the pan

2 cups Marshmallow Fluff

1 teaspoon vanilla

Boil milk and sugar over medium heat to soft-ball stage, stirring continually, about 20 minutes. (The soft-ball stage is reached when a bit of the syrup, dropped in cold water, holds the shape of a ball that flattens upon removal. Or, dip a candy thermometer into the syrup; it should read between 234°F and 240°F.) Pour into a large bowl and add the chocolate chips, nuts, margarine, Fluff, and vanilla. Mix well to blend.

Lightly butter two 9-by-13-inch pans. Pour fudge into prepared pans and refrigerate to set, then cut into squares to serve. Can be stored frozen for a month or two.

KENDALL CROLIUS

Vice President of Marketing, Forbes Magazine

My father is a wonderfully talented man who can do many, many things that no one else can do; he's just the handiest person in the world. But to this day, he will not make a peanut butter sandwich for himself. If my mom's out doing errands, he'll wait till she gets home at two-thirty P.M. so she can make him a sandwich for lunch. He's obviously smart enough and able enough that if he wanted to make himself a sandwich he would. But he likes to be taken care of, and I think that's what cooking is all about. It's primal and maternal; your job as a mother is to feed the ones you love. I also think that if you love to cook, and my mother certainly does, cooking is like giving a gift. And the best gifts reflect that you really know the recipient. Knowing how my son, Trevor, likes his beef stew, or how my daughter, Martha, likes a grilled cheese sandwich, is part of it. Martha makes a damned fine grilled cheese all by herself and doesn't need me to cook it. But when she says, "No one makes a grilled cheese sandwich like you do, Mom," I fall for it every time. It underscores and illuminates the connection that we have, the intimacy of truly knowing each other.

I think it is important to give food, and that food is significant. When I was in the advertising business, I worked on several food accounts. We talked a lot about what food means, and what it means to feed people, and all that psychological stuff. James Patterson, who now writes best-selling novels, was creative director. His way of summarizing the importance of it—and he didn't mean this in a disparaging way, because he really believed it was true, but he was a busy man and we needed to move on—was, "I love you; here's my meat loaf." As a mother, feeding your child is very basic. After you give birth, it's the next way that you give life, and sustain it, and nurture it. There's that phase where you're nursing and everything is pure and you're in complete control. The kids get a little bit older and you're shoveling in the organic baby food and you're in pretty good control. The older they get, the less control you have over what they ingest; God help you, you hope it's only food. My kids are now teenagers, but feeding them is still my way of taking care of them.

My daughter, who's thirteen years old, was diagnosed with cancer when she was ten. She's fine, thank God—she had a kind of cancer that has a ninety-two-percent cure rate. The treatment is very aggressive: surgery, radiation, six months of chemotherapy. The angst I went through in trying to get her to eat! Because in addition to nausea from the chemo, she had anorexia—not anorexia nervosa but anorexia, which is the physical condition of lack of appetite. I remember Martha saying to me at one point, "I know I'm hungry but nothing sounds good to me." And the feeling of powerlessness I had because of that. I felt powerless over so many things, but the one thing I thought I could do was make her something she would like to eat.

The oncologist said, "If she wants Cheetos, give her Cheetos. Calories. Don't worry about the quality of the food." But there was just nothing she wanted. And suddenly one day it would be Chinese food! And we would drop everything and run out and get Chinese food, but by the time we got back it would be something else. She wasn't being a princess. Things she once loved she didn't like anymore, and things she hated sounded maybe a little bit appealing. It was different every day. The worst of it was that at the end of chemo, she looked like Olive Oyl, Popeye's girlfriend, with scrawny arms and legs, and bulges for elbows and knees. It was just horrible. Now she's ravishing and fine, but that experience of not being able to create the thing that appeals and nurtures and sustains was traumatic. As a result, food became a complication. I didn't spend a lot of time compensating by cooking; I spent a lot of time compensating by trying to nurture her in other ways and totally ignoring my son and my husband.

When she finished the chemo in early November, she was feeling so much better and her appetite came back. On the Saturday of Thanksgiving weekend, we threw a party we billed the "Thankful for No More Chemo" party. We invited everybody who had cooked a meal, sent a card, brought flowers. We assumed that a lot of people would be away for Thanksgiving. Nobody declined; 150 people showed up. It was really crowded, but it was the best party I have ever been to in my life, because there has never been a better reason for a party. I was so delighted that Martha had an appetite back I was happy to cook—a big buffet with lots of hors d'oeuvre-y things, and a ham because we were all burned out on turkey.

Anytime anything like this happens to a child, everybody, even people outside your immediate circle, sees their life before their eyes and it affects them deeply. The minister of our church said a really wise thing to me. He sat me down the day after Martha's surgery and said, "People really, really, really need to help you right now. I know you're very capable and used to taking care of things yourself, but the greatest gift you can give your friends and acquaintances is to let them help you." And I thought, Okay. Nancy, our neighbor across the street, organized a food brigade. We had a big cooler that sat on the front porch, and she posted these rules we didn't know about until later: "You will *not* ring the doorbell; you will *not* say hello; you are *not* there for a visit; you will leave the food in the cooler and *get out!*" So people would tiptoe up to the porch and leave food. There were days when we felt we couldn't see anybody, and there were days we would hang out in the front parlor and wait for someone to come by: "Ooh, you brought us dinner! Come on in." People we had never met before were cooking dinner for us—a lot of lasagna, I must say, but somebody on the food brigade grilled a steak and sliced it up, and added twice-baked potatoes to throw into the microwave, and a salad. I remember that meal as a stand-out. We would still be getting dinner every night if we hadn't put a stop to it. After six weeks of the food brigade, I said to Nancy, "We're done. We're fine. We're settling back into a routine, and Martha's going to chemo only every other week." And she said, "But I still have a list of people who want to make you dinner." So we negotiated: they could make dinner on chemo days.

It felt wonderful to be taken care of in this way, and it was a real lesson, because I'm usually not good at letting people take care of me. Sometimes I really suck at it; ask my husband. I have tried to carry the lesson of it forward. The lesson was that letting people take care of you is a gift to them. By being the person who is always taking care of others I'm being selfish, and always getting all those goodies for myself. You have to reciprocate. When people cook for you in a situation like this, it's their way of saying, "I love you and I want to comfort you; I don't know what to say so the best thing I can do right now is give you soup."

My brother and sister and I grew up having wonderful things going on in my mother's kitchen. What I remember us all making together is Christmas cookies. There is *the* Christmas cookie recipe that is the same one my mother's grandparents made. I come from long lines of Germans on many sides of the family so: sand tarts. I make them now, and I try to do it with my kids and my sister's daughter and my goddaughter, because there are jobs for everyone. The mom has to roll the dough out, the older children cut the cookies and get them onto the cookie sheets. The cookies also have to be brushed with beaten egg, and sprinkled with cinnamon sugar, and then there's the coveted job of placing the piece of pecan on top. It's a whole hierarchy; you have to prove yourself to graduate to the next job. When you're really little, it doesn't occur to you that sprinkling the sugar isn't the most fun thing. You're so happy doing that and licking the cinnamon sugar off your fingers, but there's a point where you go, "Hey, wait a minute. What's that paintbrush thing called? I want to do that."

Several days before this past Christmas, I was making cookies with my sister and my daughter and my niece and talking about the whole system of it. My sister's kind of smiling quietly and looking at me, and I'm talking, talking. Finally, my sister says,

"That's great, but do you realize I'm forty-three years old and you've never let me roll out the dough?" We got absolutely hysterical about it, because it was true. I'm the older sister, and it's always been my job since I took it over from my mother. So my sister, this year, did get to roll out the dough. The cookies turned out just fine, I must say. But she rolled them out and said, "Whew, well that was fun; now I'm going to go back to supervising the pecans and the sugar." And I think I may have permanently regained control of the dough rolling.

My sister and I actually toyed with the idea of not making Christmas cookies this year: "If you can't do it Saturday, and I can't do it Sunday, next week is the Christmas pageant, maybe we don't have time, but we, by God, have to make time to do it!" It would not be Christmas without sand tarts; the whole package would just fall apart without them. There's something very reassuring about the annual repetition of it. Your sense of smell is connected to the primal, reptilian part of your brain. Smells are supposed to evoke a memory more directly and more dramatically than any other sense. The smell of Christmas cookies baking—not just eating them, but what the house smells like when you're preparing them—is half the fun. And eating the first Christmas cookie, warm off the baking sheet, and taking a cookie or two out of the tin in the kitchen all during the Christmas season. We still leave cookies for Santa on Christmas Eve, and he still eats them. One year, in a late evening daze of tidying up, I washed the plate we'd left the cookies on. My husband, Stephen, caught my mistake before we finally went to bed, and we left another crumby plate on the mantle.

Aside from making Christmas cookies, I don't remember a lot of cooking side by side with my mom. I think I learned more from watching than from standing shoulder to shoulder with her and doing it, and by osmosis. Just by being there in the kitchen, it becomes part of you. My memories of it are more that I'm sitting at the kitchen table talking while she's cooking, or I'm sitting at the kitchen table doing homework while she's cooking, as opposed to, I'm chopping this and we're doing it together. My daughter and I cook together in the sense of, Okay, you chop that and I'll wash this, and can I add this, and she likes to mix the meat loaf with her hands, which is the most fun part. I'm at ease with it all, and I think I learned that from my mother, because I've never seen her get stressed by cooking. If you know what you've got to do, it's not daunting.

People don't make casseroles anymore, but I resurrected one a couple of years ago. It was one my mother made that we all just adored. So we now have it once a year, on my parents' anniversary. They got married on December 22, and heading into Christmas we now celebrate their anniversary with Company Casserole. Who knows what issue of *Woman's Day* magazine this originally came out of. You cook noodles and put a layer of them in a dish, then a layer of cottage cheese, and cream cheese, and sour cream with scallions and green peppers, and another layer of noodles, then a layer of ground beef with tomato sauce. It's kind of like fake lasagna, although we're not a lasagna family. But Company Casserole, with a green salad, was always a middle-of-the-week meal. We'd also have hamburgers and chicken, meat loaf, pot roast; we certainly had meat—this was before the days when pasta was considered a meal. My mother was not a fancy cook. My father does not have a particularly adventurous palate, and no one in my family has ever liked anything spicy. To this day, my mother makes the best scalloped potatoes in the world. My sister and I accuse her of holding something back about the recipe because ours never come out the way hers do. Maybe it's just a case of You better get yourselves over here on Sunday night if you want scalloped potatoes. Every night after dinner my father would say, "What's for dessert?" And every night my mother would say, "Nothing."

Growing up, we always got to pick the menu for our birthdays: mine was leg of lamb, my brother's was pot roast, my sister's was lobster, and my dad's was creamed chipped beef. The other 364 days of the year, chipped beef was banned from the house because it's disgusting, but he thought it was great. We do in my family have a lot of food traditions. For Thanksgiving, we always have dried corn. It's a Pennsylvania Dutch dish. Kernels are cut off the cob and dried in the sun. You reconstitute them with boiling water so they puff up, then you cook them with lots of butter and lots of cream. The resulting dish is browner than corn pudding and has a nutty, roasted taste. We always have chestnuts in port wine, which everybody has a bite of but I don't think anyone actually likes. And then there's the annual debate about whether we should make mince pie along with the pumpkin pie—does anyone really like mince pie? And inevitably, there are always a couple of people, myself included, who say, "Yes, I really *do* like mince pie." But then you have to eat it.

We also have a New Year's Eve celebration, which started the first year my husband and I were in our house, the year I was pregnant with Martha. We decided we were going to stay home and we were each going to have our favorite food for dinner. Trevor wanted macaroni and cheese. I made homemade pot stickers for Stephen, and I think I had an expensive little tin of foie gras. The whole notion of "Let's make our favorite foods" has become a new tradition, and we make a party out of it every year. It's multigenerational, and now that everyone's kids are a little older, it's really two simultaneous parties. It's called the Pet Foods Extravaganza. The menu usually includes foie gras, lobster, raw chocolate-chip-cookie dough, pepperoni pizza, chocolate milkshakes, shrimp. It's all over the place, sit-down, course by course. The party gets bigger every year because once people are invited, they start dropping hints about inviting other people, and you don't want to cut anybody from the list.

When we first started, everybody would have a little of everything, but the kids don't want the foie gras, and I really don't need any pepperoni pizza. We have the first course at six thirty or seven P.M., and it will go back and forth—snacks for the kids, then the grown-ups will have a sit-down appetizer. We'll stop so people can wash dishes; somebody else may prepare the next course. My friend John is a hunter, and he usually brings some duck breasts. As my best friend, Annie, who lives across the street, says, part of the objective is to use every piece of great-grandmother's silver and every piece of crystal and every appliance in the kitchen. How are we going to use it all, and make it beautiful and fun? Annie gave me antique crystal sorbet glasses a few years ago, so now we always have a homemade sorbet as a palate cleanser after the foie gras course.

Dinner goes on for five or six hours, with big breaks in between courses. We print a menu in really bad French and really bad Italian. Interestingly, in the last couple of years, what's been happening with the adult menu is that we're circling in on the perfect meal. There's a foie gras dish with artichokes that we made two years ago, and everybody decided they wanted it again this year. So I think we've got our first course permanently solved.

This year's party was fantastic. There was some trauma trying to find *ras-el-hanout* and ground sumac and pomegranate syrup for the rack of lamb, which was served with roasted garlic and a date-and-lime-and-pomegranate chutney. But I managed it in the end, and it tasted unbelievable. Nancy, the Eva Braun of the food brigade from across the street, usually makes her fabulous dip, the recipe for which starts: "Open a can of Frito-Lay jalapeño dip." It's so good you can hardly stand it, but unfortunately, she couldn't come to this year's party. We made a pulled pork sandwich for the nephew of a friend who came up from North Carolina. And pasta carbonara with extra bacon and cheese; and an assortment of tapas; and osso buco with wild mushroom risotto and *gremolata*; and s'mores; and cranberry lime white chocolate tart; and that wasn't even the half of it.

Cooking and eating like this is absolutely about community. When you break bread together, you're probably not going to kill each other in the next moment; you're not going to go to battle. It's a bonding experience, and it's a ritual. That's why the Eucharist is a ritual in the Christian church—it's about sharing a meal. There's something about sharing a meal that cements the relationships you have with the people you care about. It's very profound.

My kids both have a highly developed appreciation for ritual and tradition, given that they're teenagers. There have been times when we've said, "Maybe we won't make . . ." and the kids say, "No we have to do that, we *always* do that." There is a bit of immortality in these kinds of traditions, and I would be devastated if I thought the sand tarts weren't going to go on. I was just thinking the other day about stories my grandmother would tell me, which had nothing to do with cooking, like the one about the time her dogs had the ice-cream cones: one dog liked vanilla ice cream, and the other dog liked chocolate ice cream. She had a million of these stories. I made a note to myself to tell Trevor and Martha about the dogs and the ice-cream cones, because that's as important as the cooking and the holiday traditions. It's what we do as a family and how we celebrate. And in a sense, it shows us who we are.

The kitchen is the room in almost any house that, to me, feels emotionally the warmest. I've seen some sleek, granite-countered kitchens that don't feel warm at all, but in lived-in houses they do. The kitchen is easily my favorite room in the house, no matter what house I'm in. I think it's because good things happen there, and real things happen, and it's rarely a room that's for show. So much utilitarian stuff must go on that there's a down-to-earth-ness and a practicality even in the fancy-schmancy kitchens. Maybe they absorb the warmth of all the people who have been in them, talking and eating and cooking.

Cooking is completely fundamental, and it's a part of life. Organizational skills, the ability to improvise, the ability to make the best of what you've got, and a desire to please: those are all aspects of my personality that are evident in a lot of things but that are really crystallized in the act of cooking. It is making something tangible, which for me is very satisfying because in my business I deal in ideas and abstractions. Another tradition is that for Christmas I make honey jelly for the people in my department and my colleagues. Honey jelly is just the easiest thing in the world: honey with a little bit of lemon and some pectin, so it doesn't fall off your toast. I can say, "Look, I made this for you." It's not what people think the VP of Marketing at *Forbes* is doing in her spare time. I imagine they think I'm working out at the gym, or playing golf, or doing power-something. Even today, it's somehow not what's expected of a career woman, and I like the perceived quirkiness of it.

I'm not an artist, I'm a craftsperson, in terms of how I knit and likewise in terms of how I cook; I'm not making something that's never been made before. I feel a little like Salieri in the movie *Amadeus,* in that I recognize art and true creative genius, and I know that's just not where I am. But I'm comfortable cooking, and I derive a lot of satisfaction from it because I know not everybody is comfortable doing it, and it seems to impress people. I'm very outer-directed; I need support and approval and validation. And when I cook, I get it.

• SAND TARTS •

2½ cups sugar

1 pound unsalted butter

4 cups flour

2 large eggs, beaten

1 egg white

Cinnamon sugar (see note)

Pecan pieces

Cream the butter and sugar in a medium bowl. Slowly mix in the flour, then the whole eggs. Cover the dough and chill overnight.

Preheat the oven to 350°F. Butter the baking sheets.

Roll out the dough to ⅛-inch and cut out cookies with holiday cookie cutters. Brush with egg white, sprinkle with the cinnamon sugar, and top with a piece of pecan.

Bake 10 minutes, until lightly golden around the edges. Let the cookies cool on the baking sheets before eating and storing.

Note: For the cinnamon sugar, mix ¼ cup of granulated sugar with 4 tablespoons of ground cinnamon.

• DRIED CORN •

Adapted from Better Than Store-Bought *by Helen Witty*

Serves 8

1 cup John Cope's Dried Sweet Corn (see note)
Salt
Butter
Cream (optional)
Pepper (optional)

Combine 1 cup John Cope's Dried Sweet Corn with four cups water in a saucepan and bring to a boil. Cover and simmer until desired texture is achieved, about 10 minutes to an hour. Season with salt and butter, and cream and pepper if you like.

Alternately, follow the directions on the box of John Cope's Dried Sweet Corn for Stewed Corn.

Note: John Cope's Dried Sweet Corn can be purchased online at www.caneandreed.com.

• COMPANY CASSEROLE •

Adapted from Specialty of the House: 100 Recipes from 100 Famous Cooks *by the Florence Crittenden Society League of New York*

Serves 6

1 pound hamburger meat
3 tablespoons butter or margarine,
plus extra for buttering casserole dish

2 (8 ounce) cans tomato sauce

8 ounces wide egg noodles

1 cup cottage cheese

8 ounces cream cheese

¼ cup sour cream

⅓ cup chopped scallions, green part only

1 tablespoon chopped green pepper

Preheat the oven to 350°F and butter a 2-quart casserole dish. Warm 1 table-spoon butter or margarine in a heavy skillet over medium heat and brown the hamburger. Stir in the tomato sauce. Remove from heat.

Bring 4 cups of water to a boil. Add salt and the noodles and boil until tender. Drain.

Combine cottage cheese, cream cheese, sour cream, scallions, and green pepper.

Spread half the noodles in the casserole dish. Cover with the cheese mixture, then the remaining noodles. Pour 2 tablespoons melted butter over the noodles, then put the hamburger mixture on top, patting it slightly.

Bake uncovered for 20 to 30 minutes, until heated through. Serve hot.

KATE JACOBS

Singer-Songwriter

When my sisters and brother and I were little, my mother played a game with us called Spin the Globe, which she devised because she was so bored with trying to think of things to cook for supper. She would spin the globe, and we would each get a turn putting our finger on it, and wherever it landed she would say (for example), "Oh, Ecuador!" And she would go look up Ecuador and cook some version of something from there.

My mother is Russian, and she grew up in a Russian community in Prague. When I was a girl, she made a lot of traditional Russian food, like borscht and *pirozhki,* which are little cabbage- or meat-filled pastries, and the traditional Russian Easter foods, *paskha* and *kulich. Kulich* is a saffron yeast bread, dense and sweet. We always baked it in a coffee can and made a little hat for it out of a square white cotton handkerchief dipped in icing that would become stiff. We would pick up the icing hat, slice a piece of the bread off the top, and put the hat back on to keep the bread fresh. *Paskha* is similar to cheesecake. You combine egg yolks and heavy cream and dry farmer cheese and some citron and slivered almonds, put it into a cheese-cloth, and stuff the mixture in a wooden mold that's shaped like a pyramid. The mold has a little drainage hole at the end, and you weight it with a rock and put it in the refrigerator for a few days so the moisture drains out. Then you serve it with cold ham and a bowl of red-dyed Easter eggs. It's amazing, and just ridiculously rich. One thing her mother always made on the first of March that my mother still makes are little buns called *zhavoronki*, which means "little larks" in Russian. She makes a dinner-roll dough, twists it into a pretzel to make the head and body, pulls out a point on one end for the beak, and uses whole cloves for eyes; then she brushes it with egg to make it shiny and brown. *Zhavoronki* signify the return of the birds and the coming of spring.

My mother didn't learn to cook from her mother, though. She was considered the intellectual in the family, so it was always, "Katia can't cook because she's reading. Natasha, go peel the potatoes." I think she taught herself when she became a full-time suburban housewife and mother in Virginia. She learned how to garden and how to cook, because that was all anybody did. She married kind of late for her era— she was thirty—after spending her post-college years in New York City working at the Rockefeller Institute (now known as Rockefeller University). She was a bacteri-ologist, and her father was a doctor, and her father's father was a doctor, and she's a very scientific person. But thrust into the suburbs with four children under five and everybody cooking and gardening, she really took to it. I think it was an escape for her to have a personal pursuit that was creative. Also, she told me that the only thing we would let her do was cook. We would torment her if she read; she couldn't talk on the phone. But she said as long as she was cooking, everything was perfectly fine; all the kids would play and hang around and find things to do with themselves and not harass her. It's the same with me and my kids. Cooking is a way for me to withdraw a little from the mayhem but stay close to the hearth, and my kids like it. One of my son Thomas's first sentences was, "What's the first ingredient?"

Our house in Virginia was a very tiny cinderblock ranch, and we were constantly going in and out of the kitchen from the backyard. It was easy living in those days when we were little. (Easy for us, anyway!) I remember watching my mother cook. My first memory of cooking myself was when my mother went into the hospital for two months with pleurisy when I was eight years old. She was gravely ill, I know now. Then, all we knew was that we had to do the cooking. My brother was thirteen, my two sisters were between us, and we took turns. I remember being in the kitchen and cradling the phone while my mother talked me through an Irish stew from her hospital bed. That's the first real thing I cooked that wasn't sweet: beef and carrots and onions, in an old pressure cooker my mother used all the time. It was a terrifying thing. The whistle was broken, and we had to use a knife to lift the pin on the lid to let out a loud, frightening jet of steam. I browned meat with the phone to my ear, standing on the kitchen stool to peer into the pressure cooker.

I enjoyed domestic chores when I was a child. My family is very talkative, but as the youngest, I never talked much. Cooking was a comfortable role because it was necessary, busy, involved, and I was good at it. I enjoyed being in the heart of the family and having everyone together, and I liked pretending to have a little family I had to care for. We used to come home from the Safeway with a dozen bags full of food, and I would put it all away very methodically, imagining I was running an orphanage and would be feeding an army of hungry children.

The really famous thing that happened at the time my mother was in the hospital was that my sister Lucy, who to this day is the non-cook in the family, took a casserole and filled it with raw rice, then dumped a bottle of ketchup on it and put it in the oven: that was her dinner when it was her turn to cook. I also recall my father walking to the dining room table, where the four of us were waiting for dinner, and smashing a white china soup plate full of peas on the floor. It must have been a terrible time for him. I remember it as an adventure.

My mother was a fan of Euell Gibbons. Gibbons was a naturalist, and he wrote books about foraging, like *Stalking the Wild Asparagus*. He's the person who really had her sending us out into the backyard to gather things. There's a strong foraging tradition with Russians; my mother grew up going out into the woods to collect mushrooms, and making herbal tinctures, which she still does. She puts blossoms of

Saint-John's-wort—called "beast killer" in Russian—into a jar with oil and steeps it on a sunny windowsill and uses it as a burn salve. She used to send us to pick the salad for dinner. We'd come back with dandelion greens, and wild sorrel, which I loved, and violets, which my mother candied. There was a black locust tree down the road from us that had beautiful heavy racemes in the spring, and we would climb the tree to pick them, then dip them in batter and fry them like squash blossoms. When we went to the beach, my mother would bring bits of seaweed in for us to taste. Anything that was peculiar, she was interested in.

My father had a foreign service job for six years, and during that time we got to live in Vienna. My mother entertained constantly—anything from small dinners to cocktail parties for a hundred guests. She was fearless; she'd cook for all kinds of people she'd never met, from all over the world. She had a piece published in the *Washington Post* when we came back to the States about whipping up a quick dinner: your husband called, he's coming home with a guy from the embassy in three hours, and what are you going to make? She wrote about a Greek dinner. We grew up next to a Greek family in Virginia, the Zachariases, and they taught us many of their recipes—*stifado*, which is a Greek beef stew with cinnamon, tomato paste, and pearl onions; and egg-and-lemon soup. Those recipes became part of Mom's repertoire in Vienna for fast, fabulous meals. Often we children ate with the grown-ups, if it was just a couple from the embassy and they were joining us for a family dinner. Sometimes it would be a big dinner party and we'd be off in the kitchen. It was such a fantasy for all of us. I don't think my mother was ever as happy in her life as when we were living in Vienna.

We lived in a grand four-story embassy house with parquet floors and a dramatic staircase and a formal dining room and an enormous living room, and the kitchen was huge. It wasn't at all modern, but it was big and spacious with lovely windows and high ceilings and black-and-white-checked linoleum, which to us was very glamorous after the tiny Virginia kitchen that was a little box, with about two steps from stove to fridge to counter. It was a gracious eat-in kitchen with no dishwasher, which is the most amazing thing, because we entertained so much. My mother usually washed the dishes herself, staying up till four in the morning, singing and mulling over the events of the party, replaying them in her head.

In Vienna, entertaining was part of the job. We all helped. My mother made little outfits for my sisters and me, loden green for Austria, with caps and starched aprons, and we would pass hors d'oeuvres and take coats and try to get people to tip us. For one important party for some big muck-a-muck dignitary who had a delicate stomach, my mother was nervous—somebody she didn't know who was important and renowned for being fussy. She decided to hire a woman a lot of other embassies used as a chef. The lady was very snooty and had just finished an engagement with Countess von Lichtenstein. She called the day before the party and said she'd broken her leg, but, "Don't worry, I'll send my son. Don't you know my son?" It turned out he was *the* celebrity television chef in the mid-'70s in Vienna. Then we were in a total panic because we had this TV star coming, Herr Comondo.

My sisters and I were assigned as kitchen help. The menu was: seafood cocktail; a very typical clear bouillon with sliced crêpes; roast chicken stuffed under the skin with mushroom *duxelle*, parsley, breadcrumbs, and garlic; diced cooked carrots; romaine salad with French dressing; Hungarian apple cake; and Grüner Veltliner, an Austrian white wine. A very simple, elegant meal, something my mother wouldn't have been able to cook because she was too impatient to be so restrained.

Herr Comondo came in and immediately started to make the bouillon, and he said he wanted my mother's biggest stockpot. She gave him her biggest stockpot and it had a hole in it—typical. He said, "No problem," and he took a pellet of bread and stuck it into the hole and burned it over the flame to fix it. He taught my sister Nell how to chop parsley, which she still does; she's very proud of her parsley chiffonade. My mother was so jealous—she kept running in from the dining room, poking her head in, and we'd all be laughing; he was a funny, warm man. She had made a Sachertorte (not for the party), which was sitting on top of the fridge and wasn't iced. It usually has a very glossy chocolate icing spread over a thin layer of apricot preserves, and my mother hadn't learned how to do that yet. Herr Comondo took the torte down, and in between courses, he whipped up a chocolate icing and showed my sisters and me how to ice it. My mother was disappointed she missed the lesson.

I came to love Austrian cuisine: wonderful dumplings, like *Leberknödeln* (liver dumplings), served in a clear beef broth with minced parsley, and *Serviettenknödel* (napkin dumpling), which is a big bread dumpling steamed in a napkin, then sliced and served with mushroom sauce. My mother jumped in and learned a lot about Austrian cooking. She was not intimidated by the pastries, and she learned how to make apple strudel and Sachertorte, and the multilayered meringue Stephanie Torte, and all kinds of fancy things. She just gave me her recipe for strudel, and it's a weird one. You mix flour and water until it's a gooey mess, then you dump it all on the counter and you rub it, and you keep rubbing it and you think nothing will ever happen, and then like magic suddenly it goes *blump* and comes together in a ball. Then you let it rest, and then you stretch it over a big linen tablecloth dusted with flour. You're supposed to stretch it until you can read a newspaper through it. I'm dying to try it. My mother made one last weekend, when I was home. She's eighty-two years old, and she still cooks like crazy. My dad bakes bread—he once took a bread-baking class at the Culinary Institute of America. He makes his own sponge, and uses grains from a local gristmill. He built a brick bread oven in the backyard from a pattern my mother clipped from *Sunset* magazine about thirty years ago (he had built one in Vienna, too). Some parents I know, their children worry about them because as they get older they stop feeding themselves. But with my parents, it's not a problem. The pots do tend to burn up sometimes, but they are still cooking wonderfully.

When I recently went to visit them, my father had just been in the hospital, and my mother was cooking because she was anxious. She made a dish she had seen on the Jacques Pépin–Julia Child program. She always watches it, and always forgets to bring out paper and a pencil because, she says, "It looks so easy, I'll remember it." She tore out the inside of a loaf of French bread and stuffed it with fish and rice and mushrooms and dill, sort of like a crude *koulibiaca*, a Russian dish she makes. And she made a curried soup with mussels, and an angel food cake—she had egg whites left over from Russian Easter, since she had used twelve yolks in the *paskha*. My son

Edward was totally entranced by the cake, which she decorated with violets she had candied herself.

My mother's got a big, messy kitchen, with all sorts of weird ingredients tucked away—since she doesn't throw anything out, when a recipe calls for something she'll usually have it somewhere. Over the years, she has taken various cooking classes; I guess this was sort of a '50s thing, although people seem to do it now, too. She took a cake-decorating class at the local high school when I was six or seven years old, in which she learned how to construct things out of royal icing. I remember a little cradle she made for a baby shower cake, gluing the different pieces together with icing. She learned how to make a wedding cake, and she has all the different pans and columns and pins for that somewhere. She took a Chinese cooking class in Vienna, so there are all kinds of Chinese ingredients around. I remember we had a great time making spring-roll wrappers: you make a ball of dough with flour and water (a lot like strudel, really) and wrap it around your fist. Then you heat an iron pan and oil it and smear it with the dough with one hand, and then right away peel it off the pan with the other. In her current kitchen, she had a special cabinet built that's about ten feet tall. It's packed with spices. Most of the jars are old McCormick and Spice Island bottles that have since been refilled with something else. No one knows what's in them except her. She has, I'm sure, bottles of some peculiar spice that never got used up that she's had since the '60s, which she bought in Virginia, moved to Vienna, where it sat on a shelf for six years, and brought back to Virginia, where it's now sitting on a shelf in her farm kitchen.

The kitchen at the farm is probably about the same size as the one in Vienna, but it's a farmy kitchen, not elegant. The best thing my parents did when they moved in, eighteen years ago, was to put in a six-burner Garland stove with a griddle and two ovens. My parents are exceedingly thrifty, and they were shopping around and finding used stoves for two thousand dollars. They finally found one for two hundred dollars, three miles away at a local Elks club that was closing down. The price included a hundred Buffalo china plates and soup plates and a big bag of forks and knives. We used to have a big annual apple-picking party in September, when we would use all that china and flatware. Those were great feasts. One year we made cassoulet, one year, paella. And always a big pot of vegetarian chili, bread from my dad's outdoor oven, and a dozen apple pies.

My mother still has her wedding Revere Ware, and it's in constant use. The smallest pot has lost its black handle but is still in circulation with its metal stump. She has a set of three French earthenware baking crocks, one of which she's always made scalloped oysters in. She has one Le Creuset Dutch oven, and she has a set of cherrywood cutting boards that she got when she married; they're still the main ones she uses. She has used the same wooden salad bowl all my life. Her knives are the most ancient, peculiar-looking things—they've been sharpened down to thin, odd-shaped blades. I don't think she's ever gotten new wooden spoons. Hers are stained, battered, split; she's got one that's just a half a wooden spoon, but it's good for some things, like scraping things out of the corners of pots. Her only cookie sheets are blackened and bent jelly-roll pans she inherited from my father's mother. I used to think there was something in the aging and tempering that made the pans better; now that I have Aircore baking sheets, I know this isn't the case.

My parents are living in the house where my father grew up, and there are things in the kitchen, like the china sugar bowl, that have been around since he was a kid. Every day they use a small, dented colander that must be a hundred years old. There's a general sense of ancient, well-worn-ness in their house, and I've inherited this idea that you don't need a lot of things, you need a few things and they become part of you. Tom and I registered when we got married (even though we already had two kids and had been together a long time, what the heck). I got some expensive things, like one of those big copper egg-white-beating bowls. It's gorgeous, and even though I don't know how often I'll use it, I have a strong sense that I will be looking at it every day for the rest of my life.

When I cook and eat, I like for there to be plenty; it feels generous and warm. I acutely remember my father trying to carve and serve a duck au grenadine for the family plus several elegant guests in Vienna, and there is no meat on a duck, there was nothing for him to serve. It's a funny family memory, but I have a horror of that. Soups and stews are my favorite things to cook and serve; a piece of meat or fish is boring. When I talked to the caterer for my wedding, I requested family-style service, envisioning steaming bowls on the tables and people helping themselves. It didn't really work out that way. The food was very good, but the sides—roasted winter vegetables, mashed potatoes—were heaped on large white plates, and you can't really take a hearty scoop of mashed potatoes off a plate. I wished I had brought a bunch of bowls out of the kitchen.

One of the advantages to being the cook in the family is that even though I have to make a meal every single day, it tends to be what I feel like eating. My sister Lucy is into ayurvedic theory. She has an ayurvedic cookbook that's based on your *pitta* or *vata*, or whatever. She told me, "Oh my God, I'm so *vata*," and when she makes the recipes for *vata* she feels much better. She quizzed my parents to find out what they were, and then when she was visiting, she made them some ayurvedic recipes. On the last day, she made some sort of tasty, warming chai with peppercorns and my mother said, "This is the first thing I haven't had to be polite about." I think of this as cooking and eating like a scientist. My great-grandfather, who was a renowned physician, used to dump his coffee and oatmeal and boiled egg all together in a bowl and drink it down before leaving for the office. "It all ends up together in your stomach." Eating like a scientist.

I think there's some truth to it, though, trying to get behind what you want to have for dinner: What would make you feel good? What would make you feel healthy? You feel like you need something spicy, or you need something rich, or you need to have a bowl of kale—something to do with your metabolism or your state of health. The best cooking I do is when I can tune in to some zone in the middle of the afternoon and decide what would be good to eat tonight. Something comes into my consciousness, and from there I try to imagine what would go with it, and I start to experiment. Certainly the weather is a factor. It's gotten all blustery and cold today; it's turning into a stew day. Or, not to be completely selfish and to have some empathy for how Tom is feeling, if I know he hasn't had a piece of red meat in a month I might think, "All right, it's time to go get some lamb chops." There are a lot of factors, and I actually enjoy that process of triangulating on what will be good to cook.

I probably write a song in the same way. Find a story and let the details drift together in my head. It's improvisational and intuitive—at least, the way I learned to do it is. I think cooking is creative, and you either have a talent for it or you don't. A good creative day just makes you happy, and happiness is so energizing, and you feel like you can conquer the world, and have the energy to think of cooking and making dinner. On a bad creative day, I'll call in dinner from down the street.

Sometimes I go through a fascination with a certain cookbook, and then I'll make a lot of things from it. It's a good process, because I assimilate the cookbook, what the main elements are and how they go together, and then I improvise from there. How many times have I made a roast chicken? But I love to read from somebody authoritative how to make one: Daniel Boulud, M. F. K. Fisher, Patricia Wells. I feel very classy when I make a roast chicken and an aromatic rice pudding. But really, I would like to be a more attentive and precise cook. For a couple of years, my boys had a babysitter from Suriname. It's a fascinating heritage; she speaks Dutch and Hindi and English and some other local dialect. Half her family is Hindu, half is Catholic. I kept trying to get her to explain the cooking to me. She would bring us remarkable food that was so delicately flavored, something with rice that was very distinct but not strong at all. She gave me some of her recipes, and they are precise and subtle—a quarter of a jalapeño pepper very finely diced. I'm impressed by that kind of cooking; it's so restrained. I tend to overspice things, to go for big, peasant flavors.

Richard Olney wrote *Lulu's Provençal Table* about his friend Lulu Peyraud at the Domaine Tempier vineyard. There's a long foreword describing the way of life there: the father and sons make the wine; the daughter runs the business; Lulu does the cooking. She sounds like a supremely competent person. She cooks according to what is at the market in the morning, a limited range based on local produce and fish and wine. The aesthetic is wonderful. Lulu seems sophisticated and social; she lays a beautiful table and makes it all look easy. Not fussy, but hearty, rustic food. I would like to be like her, as a hostess and a cook—cooking like breathing.

When my boys get older, I hope we can just *have dinner*. My ideal image is that I make dinner, they like it, they eat it, we all eat together. I also think the work ethic of the kitchen is important. I was brought up that way, and I think that when you have to work in the kitchen, that is how you learn. But who knows? Having these kids is a mystery. Before the first Halloween rolls around, you don't know what kind of Halloween-costume mother you're going to be. Are you going to make everything by hand? Or are you going to go to Target and buy a five-dollar costume? I think I am turning out to be the middle ground, dress-up-box type of mother. Last year, both boys were parrots—a red and a blue macaw. I made wings out of felt and glued felt feathers all over them and sewed them to the sleeves of their jackets. I don't know yet what kind of kitchen mother I will be. I hope my boys will pitch in and help when asked, and I hope that they will love food, and maybe even learn to cook.

Growing up, I had a sense of certain things being incredibly precious and rare. My dad would bring home a single mango—hard to imagine mangoes being rare and expensive, but they were—and we'd slice it up and pass it around after dinner, and each of us would have a little taste. It was so special, and so wonderful. I can't even think what the equivalent would be nowadays. At the moment, my boys are just not that interested in food. They're interested in treats, and they're very interested in cake and any homemade sweet things. The other day I was getting ingredients together to make a birthday cake for my sister. I got out the sifter and a stick of butter, and Thomas, who's eighteen months old, said, "Cake!"

Just as my mother experienced with her children, my kids will let me cook when they won't let me do something else. Maybe it's some primeval sense of being cared for. That's what your mom's supposed to be doing. Not gabbing on the phone or reading the newspaper, but cooking for you.

• APFELSTRUDEL •

Makes one apfelstrudel

FOR THE DOUGH:

2 cups flour

2 tablespoons oil

1 cup warm water

FOR THE FILLING:

½ cup melted butter

⅓ cup buttered breadcrumbs

6 to 7 apples, peeled, cored, and sliced
(whatever variety you like for pie)

½ cup sugar

1 teaspoon cinnamon

½ cup raisins

Confectioners' sugar, for dusting

Put the flour, oil, and water in a medium bowl and mix well. The dough will be very wet. Pour the dough onto a clean counter and knead it until it all comes together in a ball. Do not add flour! You can add a little water if some patches seem dry or clumpy. The dough will be messy and may seem hopeless but it will roll itself up in 5 to 10 minutes. Put the dough on a plate and cover with a warmed pot and towel for 30 minutes.

Preheat the oven to 350°F. Oil a baking pan. Spread a cloth, approximately 1 yard square, on a table and sprinkle it with flour. Begin to stretch the dough ball, putting it in the center of the cloth. Coat your hands with oil and slip them between the cloth and the dough, stretching the dough out evenly with your knuckles and the backs of your hands. It should almost cover the cloth (and be thin enough to read newsprint through). Cut off the thick edges with scissors.

Brush with the melted butter and sprinkle one-third of the surface with buttered breadcrumbs, apples, sugar, cinnamon, and raisins, in that order.

Roll up the dough. Transfer it seam-down to an oiled baking pan. You might have to bend it to make it fit. Brush the top with butter.

Bake for 45 to 60 minutes until crisp and golden.

Cool before serving.

Serve sliced, warm, dusted with confectioners' sugar, *mit schlag, natürlich* (with whipped cream, naturally).

· STACY ZACHARIAS'S *STIFADO* ·

This is a recipe from our Virginia neighbor Stacy Zacharias, who is an amazing Greek chef. Eating her food is one of my primary childhood culinary memories.

Serves 4 to 6

½ cup butter

3 pounds lean beef, cut into 1½-inch cubes

Salt and pepper

1 (6-ounce) can tomato paste

⅓ cup red table wine

2 tablespoons red wine vinegar

1 tablespoon brown sugar

1 garlic clove, mashed

1 bay leaf

1 cinnamon stick

½ teaspoon whole cloves

¼ teaspoon ground cumin

2 tablespoons dried currants or raisins

2 pounds pearl onions, peeled

Melt the butter in a large casserole over low heat. Add the beef. Season with salt and pepper and cook until the beef has lost its pink color. Do not brown. Remove from heat and set aside.

Meanwhile, in a medium bowl, combine the tomato paste, wine, vinegar, sugar, garlic, bay leaf, cinnamon, cumin, and currants. Pour this mixture over the beef. Cover with the onions. Weigh it down with a heat-proof plate and simmer over medium-low heat for 3 hours. Do not stir or peek!

Add more salt and pepper as necessary.

Serve with rice, sesame bread, and red wine.

• DR. HAMZAVI'S PERSIAN RICE •

Dr. Hamzavi was a friend of my mother's in Vienna. She was Russian, and had escaped during the Revolution by marrying a Persian man and moving to Tehran, where she eventually became the first woman ophthalmologist. She stole the famed chef of the British ambassador by offering him free ophthalmological care. She learned many wonderful Persian dishes from him and shared them with us. This one I make all the time. It is an approximate recipe; vary amounts to taste. It's a very pretty, golden brown, sliceable dish. Quite elegant.

Serves 4

1 cup white rice
1 to 2 egg yolks
2 tablespoons yogurt
2 tablespoons butter, plus more
for buttering the pan
A handful of raisins
A handful of chopped almonds
A handful of chopped prunes
A handful of candied orange peel

In a medium saucepan over high heat, add rice to plenty of boiling salted water. Simmer until tender but not mushy, about 16 to 20 minutes. Drain.

Preheat oven to 350°F. Generously butter a tube pan or a medium-size heatproof ceramic bowl.

Put ⅓ of the cooked rice in a medium bowl and mix in 1 to 2 egg yolks, to your preference, and enough yogurt to make a thick paste. Press the mixture into the bottom and sides of a tube pan or ceramic bowl.

Warm the 2 tablespoons of butter in sauté pan over medium heat. Add the raisins, almonds, prunes, and orange peel (or dried apricots or whatever you like) and sauté for 2 to 3 minutes until fragrant and blended.

In a medium bowl mix fruits and nuts into the remaining ⅔ of the rice. Spoon this mixture on top of the rice in the tube pan without disturbing the first layer and pat down lightly.

Bake for about 45 minutes, until the outer crust looks golden. Unmold on a plate and serve warm or at room temperature.

MARY KEYSER

Mathematical Statistician

I don't remember going out to eat the whole time I was growing up, even though I grew up only ten miles from where the first McDonald's franchise opened, in 1955. We lived on the north side of Chicago, near Lincoln Park, in a small apartment in the back of a National Tea grocery store, so food was readily available. My father did not eat "strange" things, so for dinner my mother cooked meat, potatoes or rice, always a vegetable—canned string beans, corn, tomatoes, baked beans, or spinach. My father generally wanted his food identifiable—the meat separate from the starch separate from the vegetable. Spaghetti was a dish that was all mixed up that he actually liked, and my mother cooked one "strange" thing just for him, which none of the rest of us would eat, and that was liver with bacon and onions.

When I was a little older, my family moved to a suburb of Chicago. There I started cooking with my mother and grandmother, and sometimes my aunt. My grandmother was a fantastic cook from Vienna, Austria. She and my grandfather had built a large, three-room home for their retirement; its bright kitchen had a small table placed under an art deco mirror with a half-naked angel painted on it. It was on this table that I would help my grandmother stretch her homemade strudel dough like a tablecloth. The dough was very pliable, and we would stretch it one way, then the other, patching as necessary, until it was so thin you could see through it. We would spread the fillings (poppy seed or apple or plum or cottage cheese) and roll them up saturated in real butter.

We would make plum dumplings, wrapping dough around whole plums, dropping them into boiling water, and when they were done, rolling them in sugar. In a fancy tube pan, we would make *kugelhopf*, a yeast cake with nut-meat filling. We'd also make *kolachkes*, which have fillings like almond paste or apricot jelly. These, I think, were my favorite. I don't have any of these recipes of my grandmother's, but much of my cooking has changed, anyway, since I was diagnosed with celiac disease about fifteen years ago. Celiac disease is a type of food sensitivity that causes intestinal distress in which the villi in the intestine are damaged by the gluten protein in wheat, rye, and barley. I cannot eat anything that contains wheat, rye, or barley— all my favorite pastries have been scratched from my diet. I am happy to have good memories of making and eating *kolachkes* and bread and cakes, but these are completely out of my realm now.

Cooking with my aunt, who lived next door to my grandmother, was quite different. She made things like asparagus strata, which was pretty to look at and tasted quite good. This was a one-dish meal baked in the oven; it included bread soaked in milk and eggs, layered with asparagus and maybe red pepper. My aunt had a modern, one-story Frank Lloyd Wright–type house of large Usonian design. At the center of the house were a huge living room and family room, separated by a fireplace/wall made of narrow terra cotta–colored bricks. The rooms had floor-to-ceiling windows that were twelve feet high and stacked side by side; the span of the whole wall allowed us to look out onto the land—there were no other homes to be seen. The kitchen was medium-sized relative to today's home kitchens. We thought it was very modern in the '50s, with its stainless steel appliances and sink, garbage disposal (rare in those days), and very large windows looking out onto the three-acre backyard.

I could always count on my aunt when I needed specimens for science class. I remember assignments calling for us to find something old in our refrigerators, and my mother never had anything. Because she entertained frequently and was not so good about either eating leftovers in a timely way or throwing them out, my aunt had a refrigerator chock-full of moldy items that had fantastic colors and textures. This is where I learned about the transformation of food into otherworldly life-forms. One item I remember, because I have grown a few of these specimens myself, was cream cheese that had languished for many months in the fridge; it had a beautiful green-blue fuzzy texture growing on it. Other things were not so good or interesting, like spoiled milk and spoiled sauerkraut. My aunt was very funny and very eccentric, but we always trusted that she started with new ingredients when she cooked for us, and never worried that she would try to use her leftover surprises.

My immediate family, my grandmother, and my aunt lived in three separate houses on five acres of shared land. In the summer, my father and my aunt grew vegetables on one of these acres: corn, beans, and the best tomatoes in the world, in the blackest, richest soil you can imagine. The downside to this was the incredible amount of hot, humid work that was needed to weed and nurture the crops. As a child, I was not tolerant of bugs and snakes; I'm a little more, but not much more, tolerant now. In August, we spent lots of time picking, cleaning, and preparing vegetables to freeze for the winter. This is when I developed my love for raw green beans—so sweet and green and crisp. My mother would admonish me not to eat them because they might cause stomach problems, but I never had stomach problems eating raw beans. I would always offer to string them and cut the ends off, so it was easy to pop one in my mouth every now and then. I would also sneak them from the refrigerator after they'd had a chance to get cold.

I have not been able to duplicate in Virginia, where I live now, the delicious tomatoes my family grew in Illinois when I was a girl. Although I try. Those tomatoes were very tart with a strong tomato flavor—nothing like the pinkish, tasteless kind you find in grocery stores. It was their acidity that made the Illinois tomatoes so different. I've always attributed the flavor to the coal black Illinois soil, although this is certainly not scientific. I am currently building a new house, and there I will have some fairly rich soil (for Virginia) and a large lot with full sun. I love to make tomato salad with sliced homegrown tomatoes, fresh basil leaves, and freshly made mozzarella. I am going to try making my own mozzarella this year, because out here in the country there is nowhere to buy it. It appears from recipes I've come across that mozzarella making is easily achievable at home using whole and/or skim milk and rennet. In addition to tomatoes, I am planning to grow tomatillos in my new garden, many kinds of squash, chili peppers, cucumbers and pickling cucumbers— who needs meat? I can't wait.

About eighteen years ago, my husband introduced me to morel hunting, and I was the most successful hunter in our group on that first try. In the middle of spring, especially if it has been wet, after a few warm days wild morels can be found along streams in the mountains and in other damp, woodsy areas. Morels are unique-looking; they have long narrow caps from two to five inches long that are honeycombed and colored beige or dark brown. It's hard to go wrong and pick a poisonous mushroom by accident. After they're picked, I soak the morels in salt water to coax out any little creatures that are living inside them. Then I dry them with a paper towel, coat them in egg, dip them in rice flour, and fry them in peanut or olive oil. They are unbelievably good.

Shortly after my father's death several years ago I quit work for a while to help my mother, who is now eighty, move near my sister. During this period, I was no longer thinking about all the wonderfully complex things I do for work. Instead, I was accommodating my mother's need to prepare breakfast (and clean up), begin to prepare lunch (and clean up), and cook dinner (and clean up), and also to think about tomorrow's meals so that items in the freezer could be taken out to thaw—plus buying food in between. I realized that all the fond memories I had of my mother's good home cooking were due to the constant attention she paid to preparing meals. I do not—could not—live that way now. My busy job is important to me because, as I mentioned, I get to think about complex things and, of course, I am making money so I can build a really cool kitchen in my new house, and maybe even a small kitchen in the basement to do some pickling and canning. My new kitchen will have plenty of counter space for chopping and mixing and serving, two big sinks so that I can clean up as I go, enough cabinet space for everyday essentials (dishes, bowls, spoons, spatulas, knives) and not-so-everyday essentials (iron skillets, various flours, condiments, soup pans). A basement kitchen will keep the heat out of the main kitchen when the time comes in August to collect vegetables from the garden and do something with them. I plan to make pickles (bread-and-butter, sweet, dill), tomatillo sauces, green beans, tomatoes, and relishes.

Nonetheless, it was wonderful to spend that chunk of time with my mother so focused on food and food alone. Even though I have a job for which I work ten to sixteen hours per day and sometimes on weekends, I always like to cook. I still have a cookbook my mother gave me as a seven-year-old that has simple little recipes in it. It reminds me that the thing I liked about cooking back then was reading about it and then figuring out the magic of it all. Cooking was putting ingredients together with a little heat or cold and, *voilà*, something (usually) good to eat appeared. It was/is challenging. It was/is social. It was/is rewarding. Good family cooking reveres honest, fresh ingredients and the skill needed to prepare fine food. It's fun to cook food if someone else enjoys it and eats it with gusto.

· SAUTÉED MORELS ·

Serves 4 as an appetizer

¼ pound fresh morels
1 egg
Water or milk
Rice flour, for dredging

Salt and pepper

Olive oil

Soak the morels in salt water for a couple of hours, then rinse to remove dirt and dry. Leave small- and medium-size mushrooms whole; cut large ones in half lengthwise.

In a small bowl, beat the egg with the water. In another small bowl, add the flour, and salt and pepper, to taste. Dip the mushrooms in the egg and water mixture, then dredge them in the flour.

Warm the oil in a skillet over medium heat until hot but not smoking. Add the mushrooms and pan-fry until the outsides are crisp. Enjoy immediately.

• SAVORY TAMALES •

I must say, tamale recipes are hard to write up, because so much is done by feel and by taste. Here is my shot at it, modified from a couple of book recipes and reflecting my own experience.

A day or two before assembling the tamales, make two fillings, one savory and one sweet.

Makes approximately 50

HUSKS

Fill a stockpot with water and soak approximately 120 corn husks overnight. Rinse well.

FILLING

3 quarts water

8 cloves garlic

1 large white onion, coarsely chopped

4 cloves

1 6-inch stick cinnamon

2 pounds pork leg or loin, cut into chunks

Salt, to taste

Bring water to a boil in a stockpot. Add remaining ingredients and cook over low heat, covered, for 2½ hours, until meat is tender. Cool pork in broth, about 2 hours. Shred or finely chop pork and set aside.

SAUCE FOR FILLING

¾ cup lard

2 thick slices white onion

12 chilies (use a combination of ancho, pasilla, mulatto, and guajillos), seeded, deveined, and soaked in warm water for 20 minutes

8 cloves garlic

1 medium white onion, coarsely chopped

1 teaspoon pepper, freshly ground

½ an allspice berry, freshly ground

4 bay leaves

1 tablespoon cumin

Salt, to taste

2 cups beef broth

Heat lard in a heavy saucepan over medium heat. Add onion slices and sauté until soft. Meanwhile, drain chilies, reserving soaking water. In a blender, purée chilies, garlic, chopped onion, pepper, allspice, bay leaves, cumin, and enough of the chili soaking water to make a smooth paste. Add mixture to lard and sautéed onions and simmer 45 minutes. Add salt and continue cooking till sauce thickens.

Add beef broth and shredded pork filling. Cook 25 minutes. Remove from heat and refrigerate till ready to assemble the tamales.

DOUGH

1½ pounds lard (or butter, shortening, or a combination)

2 tablespoons salt

1⅓ pounds fresh masa (see note)

Water or beef stock, approximately 4 cups

Beat lard with a mixer till light. Add salt; add masa in 4 parts. Reduce mixer speed and gradually beat in water or stock to form a tender dough. If still firm, soften by adding more stock, 2 tablespoons at a time. To test: a small amount of dough should float when dropped into ice water.

To assemble tamales:

Take a corn husk and spread it with about 2 teaspoons of dough down the center, taking care to spread evenly to the edges. Place 1 teaspoon pork filling in a line down the dough. Fold sides of corn husk to the center, overlapping. Fold bottom up and top down toward the center and tie with cotton string or a strip cut from the corn husk. Place upright in a steamer lined with corn husks.

When the steamer is full of tamales, cover them with more corn husks and steam over simmering water for about an hour and a half, until the dough lifts easily away from the husk. Keep water in the steamer at all times, but never let it touch the tamales.

Note: Fresh masa is made from soaked and ground hominy. Some Mexican markets sell fresh masa on weekends, or you can by it from a tortilla factory if there is one near you. Look for this label, masa preparada para tamales, *to distinguish from masa for tortillas.*

· SWEET TAMALES ·

Makes approximately 12 tamales

HUSKS

Fill a stockpot with water and soak approximately 25 corn husks overnight.
Rinse well.

FILLING

1 8-ounce package dried apricots

¼ cup toasted pine nuts

¼ teaspoon ground cinnamon

Chop ingredients fine and set aside.

DOUGH

¼ cup lard (or butter, shortening, or a combination)

¾ cup sugar

1 pound fresh masa (see note, p. 90)

½ cup lightly flavored chicken broth or milk,
at room temperature

¼ teaspoon salt

1 teaspoon baking powder

Mix ingredients together with a hand mixer until well blended.

Assemble and steam sweet tamales in the same manner as savory tamales.

NANCY KEYSER-BRYANT
Real Estate Broker

I grew up in Page County, Virginia, about ninety miles from Washington, D.C., in the Shenandoah Valley. My mom and dad owned and operated a country store ten miles from Luray (home of the Luray Caverns) in a little town with a population of less than a hundred. I call it "Ten and plum ten miles out of town, plum in the sticks." The store was a place where people came not only for groceries but also for hardware and feed for their farm animals—almost one-stop shopping. My dad often traded groceries for eggs, live chickens, and cured meats such as hams and pork shoulders. I have been to many of these meat-curing events in my life. They take a lot of time, and there is a lot of socializing that goes on. Quite often, the men drink snorks of "white lightning"; the women prepare a big meal for the day with plenty of fresh hog meat to sample.

Many of Dad's customers had no phones, so they made their orders by postcard. A common order would be for a ten-pound bag of Magnolia flour, sugar, and stock feed for livestock. Often, the cotton print bags the feed was packed in would be requested. They served a dual purpose: they were washed after the feed was used, and the ladies made dresses, aprons, and tea towels from them. Many people in our community did not have vehicles, either, and my dad had to deliver merchandise to them. My brothers and sister and I would often go with him in his pickup truck on his huckster route.

We kids loved going on these deliveries. In warm weather, we rode on the back of the pickup, on top of the feed. We got to take turns opening farm gates to get to the roads that led to people's homes. We often got to explore barns, and to see farm animals and play with pets while Dad conducted business. Mom sometimes came on the deliveries, too, and could even lift the bags of feed, which weighed a hundred pounds. She couldn't put them on her shoulder, as Dad did, but she could pick them up and carry them as if she were giving them a big hug.

I'm the middle child in a family of five children, three boys and two girls, all of us between two and four years apart, so there were a lot of hungry mouths for my mother to feed. But because of store hours, Mom did not have a lot of time to cook. Sometimes she would put a pot of dried pinto or Great Northern beans to cook on a hot plate, or in the winter, on top of the old woodstove that was used to heat the store. These beans were always cooked with a piece of ham or cured pork shoulder or fatback, and would comprise the bulk of our dinner. We were not a wealthy family, but I never thought of us as being poor. We had a lot of love from our mother, and from Dad in his own way, and we always had all the basics.

When I was young, our kitchen was very small and the only stove we had for cooking was that woodstove in the store. Mom talked Dad into expanding our kitchen into the pantry and back porch when I was about ten years old. The pantry had previously had some shelving in it, and also a table for the water pail, since at that time there was no running water in our house. Water was pumped from a cistern—a holding tank in the ground; water is gathered from rain off the roof, or hauled in by truck in the event that rainfall does not meet the demand of the family—off the back porch. Before the remodeling, there was little storage as far as cabinets were concerned, and there was no electric mixer, just the old eggbeater or a metal spoon. I remember an old twenty-pound lard can, kind of beat up with dings and dents, which held flour.

We ate a lot of hoecake. This is a skillet bread, a biscuit dough made from flour, milk, and shortening, which is formed into a ball and flattened out on a warm griddle and cooked slowly until it has risen and become lightly browned, then flipped to brown on the other side. It's great with beans: buttered heavily, dipped in the bean broth. But really, hoecake is good with anything.

Another dish Mom would prepare was sawmill potatoes. Peeled potatoes were sliced about a quarter-inch thick and cooked in water with salt and pepper until they started to get a little mushy, and then the water was cooked down and thickened; sometimes onions were added, and sometimes cheddar cheese if we had it on hand. Dad sold a lot of cheese; it was delivered to the store in big, round wooden containers. Customers would come in and buy a Coke, ask for a hunk of cheese and some crackers for a snack, and eat this while they talked about local news and politics, sitting on an old wooden bench at the back of the store. My brother Jim still has that bench.

My family's farm was about eighty acres, and it bordered the Shenandoah River. There is a beautiful rock cliff on the property that is known as Golden Rock. It has been the subject of many photos and has appeared in a magazine called *Virginia Wildlife*; it is currently on the cover of our local phone book. I have many memories of fishing, swimming, ice-skating, picnicking with my family on this spot, and also just sitting and enjoying the beauty.

We had some cows on the farm that pastured in the fields, some horses from time to time, chickens for eggs and Sunday dinners. I can remember my mom cutting off the heads of the chickens on a large block of wood, the chickens flopping around splattering blood, and the kids running around after them. After the chickens had expired, we would dip them in a large kettle of boiling water, up and down several times; this loosened the feathers. Then we would pluck the feathers out. Sometimes we would do ten or twelve chickens at a time. My dad would sell the plucked chickens to restaurants in Front Royal, a town about fifteen miles north of us. We also raised hogs now and then, which we usually sold at a local livestock auction.

Since we had cows, we had our own fresh milk and cream. Dad usually did the milking, but when I was about thirteen years old and out of school for the summer, it became my responsibility. You sure do build up your hand muscles doing this. And what an experience it is! You need a small stool or a bucket to sit on so you are low enough to be sitting under the cow's udders. Your body is right against the cow as you milk. You grab a teat in your left hand, and another one in your right hand. Then you push the bag upward with your fists and as you pull downward, you close your fingers, from your pointer to your pinky, in quick succession, squeezing tightly as you go. This pushes the milk out in a nice stream. You do this until you have milked these teats out and then you move on to the next two. Some cows milk easier than others. Usually you give the cow a bucket of feed to eat so she is occupied with eating and not concentrating on you.

You have to be careful when you milk; if you are a little rough or if the cow is ornery, she will give a good kick and knock you and the bucket over (spilled milk). At the end of that summer, when Dad took over the job of milking again, the cow kept kicking him. We believe it was because I was gentler with the milking than he was.

The reward of your labor is fresh milk and cream. Once home with the bucket of milk, you need to strain it, just to make sure you did not get anything undesirable in it, such as a fly or a piece of grass. Once it's strained, you cool it in the fridge. The cream, being heavier than the milk, will separate and come to the top. You can spoon it off to use for whipped cream, or to put in your coffee. Or just stir the cream into the milk and drink a glass. Fresh milk tastes nothing like store-bought—it's much richer.

The most common dish from my childhood was something we fondly nicknamed "Keyser Dip." This was a milk gravy that my mother made almost every morning for breakfast and often for dinner (which we always called supper) as well. The base was either drippings from fried meat such as sausage or bacon, or from lard, or a combination thereof. Often, our bacon was sliced cured pork shoulder that hung in the building beside the house, and we just went out and cut off what was needed for that meal. Our sausage was from recent butcherings that neighbors had done—usually in November, around Thanksgiving—and it was very fresh. Mom never had many extra drippings, as she used them so often, usually in the same meal she'd accumulated them in. If she didn't have any drippings, she would just use lard in their place. Keyser Dip was always prepared in an iron skillet, one of several Mom owned. Flour was browned in the drippings, milk was slowly added, cooked until it thickened, salted and peppered to taste. It was served over bread, potatoes, or just on the plate for dipping bread. The taste is similar to sausage gravy, if you have ever eaten that.

My brother Jim did a lot of hunting for the family. He probably started hunting when he was about twelve years old, and I'm not sure how he got started, as I do not recall my dad ever hunting or teaching him. Jim provided us with deer, rabbit, squirrel, and an occasional groundhog. The only two people in our family who ever ate groundhog were Dad and Jim; I could never bring myself to try it. It had a strong smell and there was a lot of grease on top of the water when it was boiled. Rabbit or squirrel gravies are excellent, though. Squirrel is all dark meat—and very little meat at that, since the critter is so small—but it has a sweetness to it. Rabbit is similar to chicken, except none of the meat is as white as chicken breast. My mother made gravies with rabbit and squirrel by parboiling the meat until very tender, and using the broth from that in place of the milk in the Keyser Dip recipe. She then browned the meat in a skillet and served that along with the gravy. Or after parboiling and removing the meat from the bone, Mom would make potpie to stretch the meat, adding potatoes, carrots, onions, and celery, thickening it all with a little cornstarch or flour, putting it in a pie crust bottom and top, and baking it in the oven.

My mom did not clean any of the animals that Jim killed. He did that; if you killed it, you cleaned it. But Jim used to coax me into going rabbit hunting with him so I would carry the game and take the load off him. Several rabbits can become quite heavy when you have to carry them a mile or two, especially if you are a little girl.

Summertime was gardening time at the farm, and then we had lots of fresh vegetables for our meals—beans, cucumbers, potatoes, onions (which I hated as a child), corn, tomatoes, cabbage, beets. We kids helped with the plantings and did the weeding and the harvesting. These were our chores before we could go to the ol' swimming hole and play with the neighborhood kids. We also did a lot of canning of the excess vegetables, made pickles and jams of picked wild blackberries, raspberries, and strawberries. My, it takes a lot of strawberries to make a quart! Wild ones are so tiny.

After the veggies were picked and strung and snapped, Mom and I would do the canning. Canning is a time-consuming process. Usually, there would be a bushel of beans to can at one time and this would take Mom and me all day, as a canner holds only seven quarts, and a bushel makes twenty quarts or so, enough for a mess for the family. We would snap and wash and pack green beans in quart jars, fill with water to one-half inch of the top, and add one teaspoon of salt. Scalded lids were placed on top and secured with the canning rings. I use a pressure canner now, as it speeds up the cooking time. But when I was a child, we used an enamel canner. We put the jars in the canner on a metal rack, added water enough to cover the jars, brought it to boil, and cooked for two hours. I now prefer freezing to canning, as the vegetables taste fresher, but I do still make pickles, and can tomatoes and tomato juice and green beans.

Since I work at my job about fifty to fifty-five hours a week, on Sunday, I will prepare a large meal with plenty for leftovers for lunches or extra evening meals: sometimes a roast—pork or beef—and vegetables such as potatoes, carrots, and onions that I cook with it. This past Sunday, we had fresh bass caught from our pond with corn muffins and oven-fried potatoes. There are fresh morels in the fridge that we found in the woods near our home, waiting to be batter-fried. We eat deer meat at least once or twice a week. My husband hunts, and we have the deer butchered by a local butcher and packaged for our needs. You can substitute deer for beef in any recipe.

I would like to entertain more, but time does not seem to permit this as often as I would like. Usually, I cook the meal for Christmas day for about fifteen to eighteen people, and have family in several other times during the year. A few years ago, my husband and I invited my brother and his wife and four of our neighbors for a prime-rib dinner. The prime rib came from a local butcher shop and was very fresh. I marinated it for twenty-four hours in a little oil, wine, soy sauce, and pressed garlic, and served it with salad, baked potatoes, and Silver Queen corn, which I had frozen in our freezer, left over from the summer. Everyone brought a bottle of their favorite wine to share. By the time we were well into the meal, the volume of voices was on high. It was a great meal with great fellowship. Special planned meals for family or friends are a way of showing that I care for them and think they're special.

I love to prepare all kinds of food, but if I had to list one that I prepare the most, it would be bread. My German ancestry, I guess. My husband talked me into purchasing a bread machine about three and a half years ago. I don't have to worry about it collecting dust, since I use it an average of two or three times a week. We buy very little bread from the store. Since the purchase of the bread machine, I have collected ten bread cookbooks and tried many of the recipes. I bake a lot of bread to give to friends, relatives, and clients. A loaf of bread makes a great housewarming gift with a bottle of wine. Usually, bread is requested of me when we have family gatherings or dinner at a friend's house. I make a lot of small loaves and freeze them, and if someone unexpectedly stops by, the bread is there to serve, or to give as a gift, or both. I'm baking some fresh bread now. The recipe today has cinnamon in it. It's divine, with its aroma of yeast and spice. The smell of fresh bread has such a soothing effect on me. It reminds me of home and family, and smiles and laughter, of love from the one who prepares it, and the love that is shared as it is eaten.

• KEYSER DIP •

If you want this dip to be thinner, just add more liquid.

Serves 4

¾ cup drippings from bacon or sausage,
or shortening or lard, or any combination thereof

⅓ cup all-purpose flour

4 cups milk, or rabbit or squirrel broth

Salt and pepper

Bring liquid to a boil, then simmer until ready to use. Meanwhile, in a medium-size skillet (I prefer a cast iron skillet) over medium-high heat, add the drippings and the flour and stir until smooth. Stir continuously until slightly browned, about 5 minutes. Slowly add liquid, and stir until bubbly and thickened, 5 to 7 minutes. Season to taste. Serve hot over bread or potatoes, or on the plate for dipping bread.

· SAWMILL POTATOES ·

Serves 4

4 cups boiling potatoes, peeled and sliced thin

1 small onion, chopped

Handful of chives, chopped

Handful of parsley, chopped (optional)

Butter (optional)

Shredded cheese (optional)

Salt and pepper

In a medium saucepan, add salt to 2 cups of water and bring to a boil. Add potatoes, onion, and chives, and cook over medium heat until they start to break up and thicken, about 10 minutes. Stir occasionally and adjust heat to maintain a low simmer until all the water is absorbed. If you like, you can add parsley, butter, and (if you are not watching calories), cheese to the potatoes once they are done. Season to taste. Serve hot.

• HOECAKE •

To make hoecake, you can use a mix such as Bisquick and follow the directions for regular biscuits, or you can make your own dough with this recipe.

Serves 2 to 4

2 cups flour

4 teaspoons baking powder

1 teaspoon salt

4 tablespoons shortening

¾ to 1 cup milk

In a medium bowl, sift together the flour, baking powder, and salt. Cut in the shortening. Add ¾ cup milk and mix. Add more milk as necessary to make a soft dough.

Grease a griddle and warm over low heat. Roll the dough into a ball and press it into the warm griddle. Flatten the dough to about 1½ inches.

Cook over low heat for about 10 minutes until lightly browned. Flip and cook the other side until lightly browned. Serve buttered, alone or with beans.

TESSA HUXLEY

Horticulturist and Executive Director,
Battery Park City Parks Conservancy

When I first started working in community gardening, I joined an organization (that I subsequently ran for many years) called the Green Gorillas. The Green Gorillas came out of an editorial in the *New York Times* written by the Vice Chair of the City Planning Commission at the time the South Bronx was burning and being razed in the 1970s. He said, "Maybe what we should do with this land is farm it." And out of that came the concept, Let's not have just rubble. Conversely, today in Battery Park City, we have a community garden that's about sixty plots. It's the highest income per capita community garden in the country, probably in the world. It doesn't matter if you're poor or rich; there's a whole segment of the population that recognizes the need to be connected to the earth in some way.

When I'm in the city, I miss having my nose in the soil. My family and I share 145 acres in Chelsea, Vermont. We have a lot of Shetland sheep, which take up thirty acres of pasture, grazing on rotation. We've had a series of tenants who got free rent in exchange for sheep care. There's no market for the wool, and we're losing money on sheep every year, but they're very picturesque and the lamb is great.

We sell some of it to restaurants and keep the meat from two or three sheep for ourselves.

The first time we ate our lamb, my kids asked, "Who are we eating?"

"This is Archie."

The next year they asked, "Are we still eating Archie?" But by then we'd moved on to the Bs.

In Vermont, we have fruit orchards and a large vegetable garden and a lot of flower gardens and some forest. My kids say, "All you do is work when we go to Vermont," but in the winter, all we do is ski. We can't really plant anything until May, except for garlic and leeks and things that don't mind the cold, which we plant in the fall. We have a huge rhubarb collection. We grow gooseberries, currants, blueberries. We haven't had that much luck with raspberries, so we've given up on them for the moment. Instead, we prowl the back roads to find wild raspberries and blackberries.

As for gooseberries, my major introduction to them was when I lived in Sweden in 1968; I was an au pair, sort of, to friends of the family. We would pick gooseberries green and cook them like rhubarb with a lot of sugar, and serve them with a little cream on top. That was one of those summers you can't really believe ever happened; it now seems like such a fantasy to me. The family I lived with had a huge farm in the west of Sweden, a couple of hours from Uppsala. It was a wonderful place. The house was built in the 1600s, so it was small, and there was no electricity or water. There was a root cellar built into the hillside that you could walk right into. The family rented out a chunk of land to a dairy farmer, so we always had fresh milk and made our own yogurt. They owned their own lake, with an island in the middle of it. We'd walk to the lake, and row a boat out to the island with a picnic, and lie on the rocks and swim and eat. I've never eaten more cherries than I did that summer. There was one mature cherry tree on the farm, and five of us eating cherries straight from the tree—we could not eat enough of them.

I have cherry trees in Vermont, too, although I haven't had much luck with them; and hazelnuts, and apples. I make mountains of applesauce, and pies, and pressed apples for cider. In Vermont, where everyone has apple trees, there are cider mills, so you bring in your apples in October and they'll squash them for you. My husband and I and the kids can pick enough apples—several bushels—to keep us in cider for a year. We have some particularly good trees for cider. The apples are little, and they're delicious for eating, but boy, cider from them is staggeringly good. There used to be several hundred types of apples grown in this country in the eighteenth and nineteenth centuries. Some of the farmers will tell you that they were about to cut all the old trees down and it's only the farmers markets that saved them. If you could get the old apple varieties back in circulation—and there are places that are working very hard at growing them—there would be a market for them. It's just a matter of getting them to the right place at a price people can afford. What I think is sad is that they aren't using those apples to make cider, and the cider you buy at the markets is too sweet, as far as I'm concerned, and doesn't have a lot of flavor, which is pretty typical of modern apples. By comparison, the cider we produce is a grand thing. It's spicy and super flavorful. I freeze about twenty gallons of it. Of course, I have an extra freezer—how does one live without an extra freezer?

I will spend far more money at the farmers market than I would in a grocery store; I'm trying to support local farmers there, and it's important to do so. I'm a member of the Community Food Security Coalition, which is a group that's trying to make the point that if you don't continue to have farming close to centers of population, you do not have food security should the unthinkable happen, whatever the unthinkable is. You don't want your food coming from California, for instance, if you live in New York. You can look at it from the doomsday point of view, or you can look at it from the point of view of wasting resources.

I'm also quite involved in a group that has the concept that there should be many seed banks, and they should be local. In this country, the National Seed Bank is in Fort Collins, Colorado. There's nothing wrong with Fort Collins, except that if there's ever a nuclear war, the bombs are going there because that's where our nuclear arsenal is. But on top of that, Fort Collins has a very particular environment. You have to grow out seeds every few years to keep them viable as they age, otherwise you get fewer sprouts. In addition, the seeds are going to adapt to whatever climate you grow them in. Instead of growing things that do well in New England *in*

New England, everything's being grown in Fort Collins. If you're interested in horticulture, this is a terrifying thing.

I feel like I was the first passionate gardener in my family. I had my own roof garden growing up, where I grew tomatoes, basil, and dahlias. I've also always loved cooking—I often describe cooking as my favorite sport—and I come from a family of cooks. My first stepmother developed cancer and decided to change careers and to do all the things she had always wanted to do, because maybe she was going to die. She lived about fifteen more years, but in that time she developed a career as a food writer. She had a column in the *Washington Post* called "Table for Eight." It was a great column, based on the premise that eight is a nice number for a dinner party.

A cookbook eventually came out of it. There was a chapter for every month, and every month she started with something you could make that would keep going— like lemon pickle or homemade vanilla. She'd gotten a postcard from a friend of hers who was a very wealthy art collector who'd taken cooking classes at the Cordon Bleu for a week and wrote, "Judy, this is great: take a bottle of not very good cognac and add a couple of vanilla beans to it, then forget about it for six months and it's the best vanilla you'll ever have." So of course, Judy went ahead and did it. Years later, when this woman came over for dinner, Judy made whipped cream with vanilla.

"This is very good."

"This is your vanilla."

"What are you talking about?"

This is how Judy knew her column had really caught on: a friend of hers who runs a wonderful kitchen store in Arlington, Virginia, called and said, "We had a bake sale at school and everyone made Palm Beach Brownies," which had been one of the recipes in her column that week.

Judy and I cooked a lot together. She would come to visit me on a fairly regular basis without my father, and we would go on food expeditions—Indian food shopping, for example, because she had lived in India and enjoyed the cuisine, but my father just hated it.

My mother is also a good cook. She's a filmmaker, and in the late '70s, she had a loft, where she started showing films on Sunday nights. The get-togethers were pretty lively affairs. There was a screen that pulled down from the ceiling, and a 16mm projector, and people brought their latest work to show. It became an event where freelance filmmakers came to get jobs. So the New York State Council on the Arts gave my mother grants to pay for the wine and the cleanup afterward. People would bring food, and inevitably someone would say, "I'd really like the recipe for . . . " And out of that came the *New York City Filmmakers' Cookbook*. It never got bound or anything, but everybody got a photocopy.

There are recipes in the cookbook that say, "If you have any questions about this recipe, call this number. If you have any work, call . . ." I still make things from the book—green tomato chutney, because in Vermont, where tomatoes are always dicey, we get a lot of green tomatoes. I make a mushroom soup from Judy's cookbook, with dried mushrooms, fresh mushrooms, altogether too much cream, milk, onions, sherry, chicken broth. Chicken broth is a critical ingredient for mushroom soup and many other things. I make enough chicken broth so that I don't have to buy it. I save all my chicken bones and when I have two large Ziploc bags of them, I make broth. Why throw out chicken bones if you can use them again? Toss them all in the pot with lots of vegetables. I'm sure I don't do it the "right" way. Some people say you should use the whole chicken, but I generally eat it first.

My husband, Andy, his sister, and several of my sisters-in-law have just finished a new cookbook, called *Eating Under the Family Tree*. It has 250 recipes in it, but partly this is because we have four recipes for chocolate roll, because Andy's mother thinks her recipe for chocolate roll is better than Judy's, but likes the directions in Judy's cookbook better. We really are a family that shares recipes. Recipes bring back memories of events, of people. Since food has smell to it, our memories of it are really evocative. Sometimes the food we remember was good largely because of the company; Judy once had dinner at the house of a friend of hers in Washington and I asked her how it was and she said, "Fabulous! The food was ghastly but I had such a good time." But sometimes the food and the company come together, and those are the recipes that become important.

I mostly am a cookbook person. It's habit, I think. I was taught to cook by a person—my mother—who always used recipes and cookbooks. If you are my child, you're going to see a cookbook open, or a *Cook's Illustrated*, or something. And you're going to probably think to cook that way, too. We follow people's habits. It's like anything else. If all your parents eat is take-out food, that's what you're going to eat. Unless you really hate it, in which case you will only use the purest ingredients. People react to what they know, either in open rebellion or by following along because they like it. A person whose mother was a terrible cook but who likes to cook themselves, has probably had some experience in their life that changed everything. My mother grew up in Pittsburgh, and she talks about discovering green salad as opposed to the Jell-O molds that are known out there as "salad."

I especially like cooking with other people. My husband likes to cook with only one other person, our very close friend Bob, who bullies him into cooking together. For my fortieth birthday, we had a ravioli contest—how many different kinds of ravioli could we all make? It was Bob's idea. We had fifteen people for dinner, and we probably had about six different kinds of ravioli. It's not that big a production. Roll it out, and then all you have to do is make your stuffing, and it's a relatively small amount of stuffing. Ravioli is a great thing to make with a four-year-old on a rainy afternoon. When you can't go outside, cranking becomes a good activity, a good substitute for Play-Doh.

I like cooking with other people because I like doing most things with other people. I don't dislike being by myself, but I find that I think better when there are other people around. I feel that one plus one is far better in almost anything. That's just my makeup. I'm always looking for community. I didn't have a large family growing up. It was just my brother and me, so I imported people to be family. My husband comes from a very large family; I'm not sure he feels the same need. I also think he's more of a perfectionist than I am. He'd just as soon buy all the food, cook the meal, set the table, eat and then let someone else clean up. I can't understand it.

When Andy and I got married, we didn't have a big wedding; we had four parties—one in New York City, one in San Francisco, one in Washington, D.C., and one in Syracuse, New York. In New York, we asked friends who are bakers to make their favorite cakes. My mother made a chocolate cake, and that was great because she bought marzipan fruits and other decorations and put them around it, and all the little kids who came to the party got to slap them on. In San Francisco, we had a tea party for a hundred. Washington was lunch outside in my father's garden.

In Syracuse, we had a clambake. We trucked in clams, steamers, and lobsters. And salt potatoes. Syracuse is called the Salt City because of its underground salt deposits. There's a tradition in Syracuse and as far east as Long Lake in the Adirondacks. You buy a five-pound bag at the supermarket that has four pounds of mature potatoes in it—they are clearly reject potatoes, because they're small and it's a pain in the ass to peel them, and they're always white of no particular variety—and one pound of salt. You put two quarts of water in with the salt and boil the potatoes (unpeeled). There are instructions on the outside of the bag that show that you open the potato, put a blob of butter on it, and pop it in your mouth.

It's important for people to understand how the world is put together. Most people in our society don't know how to sew a button on their shirt, let alone how a garment is made. I'm not saying we should make all our own clothes, only that we should know what goes into making things so we can appreciate them and not go and buy all our stuff at Wal-Mart, where workers are so exploited they can't live on the wages of a full-time job. If you know what it takes to make something, you're willing to give value to it, because if you've ever made a shirt, you know it takes time. It's the same thing with a meal; if you don't make it yourself, if you buy McDonald's all the time, how can you have any appreciation for it?

I think that people who consider cooking drudgery don't particularly like food. If it doesn't interest you, of course it's drudgery. A woman who works here at Battery Park City was saying a couple of years ago how shocked she was when a friend of her son's came over to eat and he'd never used a real plate and a fork and a knife—he'd always had take-out food. He was ten years old. I can't even imagine it. I mean, take-out food is good, but it pretty quickly becomes all the same. There are a lot of people in this world who don't cook. And there are a lot of apartments in Manhattan that don't have kitchens, and don't have dining tables.

Part of the reason society is falling apart is because people watch TV, with dinner on a tray on their knees. One of the decisions Andy and I made when we had children was that we weren't going to have a television, so there wasn't that option to fall into. Dinner should be social time. Otherwise, how the hell do you know what your children are doing? Dinnertime in our house is pretty wild. Often a fight or two. There isn't any earth-shattering conversation that goes on, but there is conversation. I'm trying to get the children to stick with conversation and not sing songs, which they are involved in at the moment; I don't know whether it's just to annoy us or what. Dinner doesn't go on that long, but it's a time when everybody sits down together and there's an opportunity for people to talk about whatever they want to talk about.

When I first started doing community programming at Battery Park City, we decided we would go for small events, with the idea that people could meet each other and talk. We have lots and lots of dancing here—line dances, square dances, circle dances—and it's all about connecting people. We have events with as many as a thousand people, but they still tend to be events that mix people up and give them the opportunity to talk to each other. I think a meal is just a smaller version of this, no matter what you're eating. As long as you're sitting together around a table.

• GREEN TOMATO CHUTNEY •

Adapted from The New York City Filmmakers' Cookbook

Makes 2½ pints

2 pounds firm green tomatoes, well washed

2 tablespoons salt

1½ to 2 teaspoons chili powder

½ ounce ginger root, peeled and minced

½ pound brown sugar

1½ to 2 teaspoons garam masala

15 cloves garlic

12 ounces malt vinegar

1½ teaspoons caraway seeds (optional)

Cut tomatoes into small pieces and put into a medium-size bowl. Sprinkle the salt over the tomatoes and let stand until their water is extracted. Pour off the brine.

In a small saucepan, put tomatoes, chili powder, ginger, sugar, garam masala, garlic, vinegar, and caraway seeds, if using. Cook over medium heat for 30 minutes, stirring frequently and crushing tomatoes slightly as they cook. Cool before storing.

• DOUBLE MUSHROOM SOUP •

Adapted from Table for Eight *by Judith Huxley*

Serves 8

1½ ounces dried porcini mushrooms

10 tablespoons butter

3 pounds fresh mushrooms, cleaned and sliced

4 large onions, sliced

3 cups condensed chicken broth

6 cups milk

2 cups heavy cream

Salt and pepper

1 cup full-bodied sherry

Rinse the porcini mushrooms quickly under warm water, put in a small heat-proof bowl, and pour boiling water over to cover. Set aside and allow to soften.

In a large sauté pan melt butter over low heat until it foams. Add the fresh mushrooms and cook, stirring, until they give out liquid and the liquid cooks off. Turn heat to low and add the onions. Cook until soft and transparent. Do not let them color.

Put the mixture into a food processor and, with the motor running, add half the chicken broth. Process until mushrooms are puréed. Put the mixture in a large saucepan with the remaining chicken broth, milk, and cream.

Strain the liquid from the dried mushrooms through a cheesecloth into the liquid in the saucepan. Cut the softened dried mushrooms into slivers and add to the saucepan. Season with salt and pepper to taste.

Just before serving, add the sherry and heat through.

ANNA LAPPÉ

Food Activist and Coauthor, Hope's Edge

I wrote *Hope's Edge* with my mother, Frances Moore Lappé, who is the author of *Diet for a Small Planet*. Our book is about courageous, everyday people who are creating sustainable communities and fair economies in eight different countries around the world. The project brought me into contact with people in the food world in a way I never was before. Recently, I went to the opening of a friend's sustainable wine bar. The place was packed with food writers from magazines like *The New Yorker* and *Gourmet*. One of the writers was telling a captivated audience about an article he'd just written about Scotch. Everybody was on the edge of their seats, fascinated. It made me realize that my entry point into food and the way I'm passionate about it isn't like that. I was excited about the idea that my friend is a pioneer of a place that supports local farmers and that she's not serving wine made from grapes that have been drenched in pesticides. But people who are passionate about food don't necessarily know about the politics of food, or want to talk about the relationships between food and community and politics and economics. Even though all of us at this bar were attracted to the same event, I felt so out of place. I didn't want to stand around and talk about Scotch, or how moist the chocolate cake was. It had never dawned on me before that you could *just* talk about chocolate cake.

For me, food is about more than, What does it taste like? My entry point to talking about chocolate, for instance, is the Fair Trade movement. How can we as consumers in the United States support cocoa farmers halfway around the world in a way that bolsters whole communities and not just middlemen filling their pockets? We think of something like chocolate as benign; most of us don't associate it with slavery. But much of the chocolate that is produced around the world is made in slavery-like conditions. So even with something like chocolate cake, I'm always thinking about how it got to my plate. There's a whole long link that takes me from cocoa farmers in Guatemala, to the people in upstate New York who raised the eggs for the cake. Taste, and texture, and is the chocolate cake moist—this is only one level.

I met a professor of rural sociology in Madison, Wisconsin, whose whole work centers on farmers. We were standing in cornfields, where the water was completely contaminated with Atrazine, a weed killer, and he was saying that for him, knowledge changes taste. That really stuck with me—the idea that taste isn't objective. Knowing where my food came from, and knowing what went into bringing it to me, can affect the way I taste it. I don't eat meat, but I've been following the whole mad cow scare. The beef we ate a week ago may have tasted fine then, but having new information about how we feed these animals changes the way it tastes to us. I can't imagine anyone reading John Stauber and Sheldon Rampton's book *Mad Cow USA* and not thinking about mass-produced American beef differently.

Another aspect that affects taste is actually knowing the people who grow your food. During harvest season, I pick up a box of produce every week through a Community Sponsored Agriculture (CSA) program in my neighborhood. The eighty families who are part of my CSA know the farmers, and also how the season has been for them. When I eat the vegetables and fruit they've grown, I picture everyone from the farm, digging in the dirt. So when I eat, there's a whole other meaning for me, a whole different connection, than if I were to open a box of some processed product. CSAs are also keeping a diverse selection of foods alive, foods like rutabagas and kohlrabi, which most people don't even know what to do with anymore.

Before writing *Hope's Edge*, I was a classic young American. I went off to college and never really cooked for myself, even though I tried to eat healthfully. I shared my mom's political views, but I thought it was enough to buy Amy's macaroni and cheese as opposed to Kraft, and I thought, Now I'm really with her program, making a difference. I'm typical of my generation: my mom cooked for my brother and me all the time, but I never integrated cooking into my life. My friends would always tease me because whenever I had people over for dinner, I would make a mess and in the end we'd sit around eating hummus and pita. But when I was working on *Hope's Edge*, which along with documenting my mother's and my journey around the world includes a hundred pages of recipes from vegetarian chefs and restaurant owners, I felt like I would be such a hypocrite if I never cooked anything from it.

At the time, I was living off and on in Paris with my partner, Eric. It was there that I learned what a complete pleasure cooking can be. We lived two blocks from an open-air market that was open every single day. Eric is an amazing cook and had been going to this market for a long time. He had his favorite vendors and knew how to pick the right things at the right time. Shortly after I arrived in Paris, he went away for about a week and I went to the market on my own. I was so proud to be picking out my fruits and vegetables for the first time. I got home and was completely demoralized. Half the fruit had already gone bad, and the melons were flavorless. I had an apprenticeship with Eric when he came back; he had to instruct me. But two years after living in Paris, I picked up some fruit at a market here in the States. I was excited to have fruit for breakfast—a mango. I was cutting it open and it was not ripe at all. I later joked with Eric that I still had a lot of learning to do. I said, "Look, this is inedible. You didn't teach me!" and he said, "I thought I had." For him, it's obvious when fruit is ready, because he grew up in a country where being in touch with your food is second nature. He knows just the way a ripe avocado feels, and the specific smell of a perfect melon.

In Paris, I started cooking recipes from *Hope's Edge*, and I had a total conversion experience. I felt like I was exploding all the myths I had around food, which I didn't even realize I'd been harboring: that I couldn't afford to cook; that it takes too long. I realized that ultimately it didn't take more time. Or sometimes it did, but that was fine—it was time I so loved having. I realized that what was fun about cooking was the alchemy of it, the science-experiment aspect. For the first time since graduating from high school, I felt like I was eating my mother's *Diet for a Small Planet* diet: lots of fresh fruits and vegetables and whole foods and grains. I can't claim that the open markets in Paris are organic, and it's rare to find the farmers themselves selling their own produce, but still, this was a huge step for me. Over time, I got to know the vendors at the market, and my favorite guys would tell me what was good that day. I lost fifteen pounds. I wasn't intending to, but I think that was my body's way of saying, "Thank you; this is what I wanted to be eating all these years. This is what's natural to me." I'd wake up and I would crave broccoli, and I'd know, okay, I'm going to eat broccoli today.

There are lots of clichés around food and one of them is: food made with love tastes better. It's a sentimental idea, but there is a lot to it. I served the meals I made in Paris—all vegetarian—to very skeptical friends. They would agree to come for dinner with the caveat: "Just don't be offended when we go out for a *real* dinner after we come to your place." But these were meals made with love and intention. And not only did I know (mostly) where the food came from, but I also knew who created the recipes: *Moosewood Cookbook* author Mollie Katzen, and Alice Waters, who owns Chez Panisse restaurant in Berkeley, California, and Annie Somerville, who opened Greens Restaurant in San Francisco. One night, right in the heart of watermelon season, we had six or seven friends over for dinner and I cooked one of the meals from *Hope's Edge*. This included a cold watermelon and ginger soup with cardamom cashew cream drops from the Millennium Restaurant in San Francisco. The flavors were extraordinary. And by the end of the meal, fully satiated, my French friends were actually applauding.

I came to cooking for myself a bit later in life than some people, but I have wonderful memories of being with my mom in the kitchen and helping her, even though I didn't know at the time how all the pieces were adding up. I think my mother showed me a great example of how you don't have to have all the time in the world to cook good food. For most of my childhood, she was a single mother and worked long hours. The conversations she and I would have about how we were doing and what our lives were like would take place in the kitchen while she was preparing dinner. Of course, many of my favorite meals from growing up are classics from *Diet for a Small Planet:* our friend Claire Greensfelder's minestrone soup, or a cheesy Mexican casserole made with layers of corn tortillas. For special occasions, my mother often made "The Thinking Person's Cheesecake"—"Thinking Person's" because yogurt replaced high-fat cream cheese.

My mother has always said that looking at food allowed her to ask some of the biggest questions about how our economic system works: what is fair, what is just. Food played a central role in her work. And she modeled for us the importance of taking the time to have meals together as a family. For most of my childhood, she would get up every morning and make breakfast for my brother and me—oatmeal, eggs, French toast with cottage cheese; to this day I can't eat French toast unless I have it with cottage cheese, just the way my mom used to make it. It never seemed like cooking took time away from her day. Rather, it was part of her daily cycle. Her way of cooking was about nurturing, and it was about having a strong home—the idea that home is the ultimate safe place, a foundation that allows you to stand up for yourself. My mother took time for us each morning, rather than just yelling, "Get out of bed! It's seven thirty-five, the school bus comes in ten minutes—you have to hurry!" Waking up, we knew there was someone to help bring us into our day, and we had the sense that every day had potential, and that every day could be a fresh start.

I also experienced the power of food and family when I lived in France. The first time I went there, I was thirteen years old and I stayed with a family. On Sunday, they took me to a family dinner. We ate a meal at this long table. I'm sure it's an exaggeration, but it really felt like the meal lasted from noon till ten at night. I barely spoke French at the time, and at one point, I didn't understand enough to realize what was happening—I thought we were leaving to go home. We *were* going home, but only to change and come back, and then the meal continued, on and on, and I was so full, and the family talked and talked and talked. I'd never experienced anything like it. This was taking the concept of food and family another step: not only do you eat meals with your family, but time is of no matter. You have wine with your meal, and for me, drinking wine is like being on vacation, it's so very celebratory.

When I later lived in France with Eric, we would have Sunday meals with his family. These were very classic French meals that started with crudités and ended with a plate of cheese. They lasted for hours and hours, and were the most precious, lovely events. When I was growing up, my family didn't have such marathon meals, but I do remember dinners, when everyone was together, as some of our happiest times.

In college, I moved from place to place, and none of my friends had homes where we had dinner together. And after I left, there were many years when I didn't have a home base. I thought, Well, I'll cook meals when I'm not living in a funky, falling-apart apartment that I just sleep in and spend the rest of my time somewhere else. I felt that there was a connection between cooking and having a home, and for a long time I didn't feel like I had a home that was my own, and until I did, I didn't want to put time into that space. I spent a year after college teaching on a fellowship in South Africa. I was also a dorm parent, living with the girls and eating in the cafeteria with them. All the meals were prepared for us, and we had no kitchens to make our own food. We were served the most unhealthy things you can imagine—vegetables boiled to the point where they had no nutritional value at all, with added sugar and oil. I saw what it did to the girls we were teaching, who were going through puberty, and to us. We all got fat and we watched, helpless, as it happened to our own bodies. It wasn't until years later, when I was living in Paris, that I felt I had more of a home, in addition to having my own kitchen and living close to the market. And that's been a critical lesson for me: whether it's really thinking before you move into a new place about where you'll shop, or taking the time to stock your kitchen so that you always have the basics on hand, we can diminish the pressures of cooking that make it so hard for us to eat well.

When I was growing up, my mother's and father's houses were diametrically opposed when it came to food. It was good for me to have the experience of both, so I could make my own choices about what I wanted to eat. My brother and I would go visit my dad in Sacramento, and he'd take us to Denny's for dinner, and we'd eat cornflakes with vanilla ice cream. At my dad's house, we had Lucky Charms and Cap'n Crunch; at my mom's, we had granola in glass jars with no brand names. I remember loving all my mother's jars filled with grains and flours and spices; she never had any boxes or brands or plastic, just whole food. I can picture our kitchen and its butcher block island with the jars on the shelf beneath it with flour and barley and rice inside, and the beauty of it. It felt so right—it was just food. I loved the aesthetics of my mother's kitchen when I was a kid, but looking back, I think there was something so attractive to me about having that direct connection to food that wasn't filtered by advertisers who have done market research to find out what's going to tantalize you into buying their products.

I think we are cutting ourselves off from a real connection to nature, and this is part of our global desensitization. A lot of the food we're eating, we don't even taste any more. We eat processed food that has a lot of fat, a lot of salt, a lot of sugar. People no longer taste real flavors. I've met people in the Slow Food movement, and they have something called the Ark of Taste, like Noah's ark, where they induct food varieties that are disappearing, like certain kinds of tomatoes. So many people don't even remember what a real tomato tastes like.

I like Slow Food's idea that we should feel passionate about flavors. I went to a potluck dinner in Wisconsin where farmers were invited to bring food they'd grown. One of them brought heirloom tomatoes. Heirloom tomatoes have been positioned as this very elite, privileged, high-ticket item. That's one way to look at it—they can be pretty expensive. But the other way to look at it is symbolically: this is an example of what you lose when you move toward a system in which economies are monopolized by corporations, and industrial farming has destroyed so much of our land. The heirloom tomato is just the tip of the iceberg. You're not just fighting for a yummy tomato; you're fighting for this whole other way of life, of what could be, of what we could have. Before that potluck, I don't think I had ever eaten a real ripe tomato in my life. I'd just eaten the standard red tomato that over the years has deteriorated in flavor—mealy, unappetizing. The idea of biting into a tomato and not having it be in the form of thin slices with mustard and pickles and lettuce and cheese in a sandwich was unfathomable. For me, that was symbolic of the loss we have experienced—the pleasure of a flavor that your mouth isn't used to; the surprise of something new, and of possibility.

More and more people are coming around to food justice issues: it's important to keep farmers on the land, it's important to improve access to food, but it's also important to ensure that people have the resources to prepare that food, and enough money to buy it. When I was in graduate school, I went to a store called Fairway for the first time. I was adding up all my groceries as I went, but when I got to the cash register, the total was double what I had estimated. I said to the cashier, "Ma'am, I'm sorry, you must have made a mistake." I was so perplexed about how this could have happened. And of course, it was because I had been shopping at a food co-op and gotten used to those prices. That's an option for some of us, but the whole movement is struggling in the face of things like Whole Foods Market. I was interviewed once by someone who said, "My friends and I, we don't call it Whole Foods, we call it Whole Paycheck, because by the time you're through shopping you've used your whole paycheck." Not only is this unfortunate because it makes whole food inaccessible to so many people, but it's also helping create the idea that organic, healthy food is only for wealthy people.

A lot of the places I've traveled to to speak about *Hope's Edge* are places where the community that's brought me in has been very connected to these issues. As a result, I've had some amazing meals. My mother and I visited Eckerd College in St. Petersburg, Florida, and the students put on a three-hundred-person organic dinner from a local farm in our honor. There were big salads with different lettuces, and the main course was tofu cut into thin strips with perfectly fresh and crispy snap peas and soy sauce. It was so delicious. The misconception that the multi-million-dollar food business wants us to have is that you can't buy a zucchini and cook it and have it taste good; you have to buy something that's been processed. They have a major interest in getting us to eat out of the box; it's where their profits lie. It's no wonder sixty-four percent of Americans are overweight or obese. When it comes to food, we Americans are so out of step with the rest of the world.

This American diet has emerged so quickly—in just one generation, we've seen the epidemic of obesity grow. Before I traveled to Bangladesh, India, Brazil, and Kenya for *Hope's Edge*, so many people I know said to me, "Oh, you're probably going to get sick; you're going to get some stomach virus." But I have never eaten better in my entire life. We were eating with people who had just picked the food they served us, and who had cooked it themselves. In India, I was taught about their understanding of the different food groups. It's nothing like ours. They are interested in the energetics of food: What foods have heat-producing or cooling effects? What foods are going to make you sleepy? What foods are going to fire you up? It is a totally different understanding of how food affects our bodies.

It's funny how you can get used to something and can't imagine otherwise. For a long time, I ate on the run. Because I work out of the house right now, it's easy to cook for myself and say, "Nobody needs to eat like that." But I have a lot of friends who get home from work at eight or nine P.M., and leave their apartments early and don't make themselves lunches, so I understand how hard it is to eat well. I think back to when I rarely sat down and had a meal in front of me, and was always throwing stuff together. Now it's a natural part of my day to use mealtime to take a break, to pause. The irony of our fixation on efficiency and working really hard is that we do a lot of things that are not efficient. When I do take breaks instead of saying, "How many hours did I put in today?" or "I only took five minutes for lunch today," the quality of the work I do is much better. We have so many issues that come up around food. We want to slip food in, get on with our "real" lives.

I just came back into town from a trip and I've got nothing in my refrigerator; I had old cereal for breakfast. For me, the past couple of years have been a process of being open to learning. These food questions have always been in my head, and in the past I was very analytical about them, rather than practicing them in my own relationship to food and eating. As I've connected more with my own diet, these ideas have gone from my head into the whole of my body. Now, as my life speeds up, I need to continue to remind myself of the importance of taking the time to cook, to eat, and to enjoy food. I need to take the time to go shopping today when I feel like I've got so much else to catch up on.

• ENCHILADA BAKE •

Author's note: *In testing this recipe, I simplified the ingredients to reflect my own taste, omitting the black olives, chopped green peppers, and canned corn niblets given in the original. Of course, if you like, you may add these ingredients back into the mix, sautéing them with the beans and the tomatoes.*

Adapted from Diet for a Small Planet *by Frances Moore Lappé*

Serves 4

Vegetable oil
1 onion, chopped
1 clove garlic, minced
1½ cups cooked kidney or pinto beans, drained
1½ cups canned or fresh crushed tomatoes
1 tablespoon chili powder
1 teaspoon ground cumin
½ cup red wine
Salt
6 to 8 6-inch corn tortillas

1 cup Monterey Jack cheese, grated

1 cup combined ricotta cheese and yogurt

Preheat oven to 350°F. Lightly oil a casserole dish.

In large skillet heat the oil over medium heat. Add the onion and garlic and sauté until soft but not brown. Add the beans, tomatoes, chili powder, cumin, wine, and salt to taste and simmer over medium-low heat for 30 minutes.

In a small bowl combine the ricotta with the yogurt. Put a layer of tortillas in the prepared casserole dish. Top with layer of sauce. Sprinkle with 3 table-spoons cheese, and dot the top with about 3 tablespoons of the ricotta cheese–yogurt mixture. Repeat layers, ending with a layer of sauce. Top with a little ricotta cheese–yogurt mixture.

Bake for 15 to 20 minutes until bubbly and serve hot.

• THE THINKING PERSON'S CHEESECAKE •

Adapted from Diet for a Small Planet *by Frances Moore Lappé*

1 pound cottage cheese or part-skim ricotta cheese

1 cup plain yogurt

3 egg whites

1¼ teaspoon vanilla

⅓ cup honey

1 unbaked dessert pie crust, spread in a 9-inch pie pan
(store bought or homemade)

Fresh berries, for serving

Preheat the oven to 350°F.

In a large bowl, put the cottage cheese, yogurt, egg whites, vanilla, and honey. Blend until smooth and pour into the pie crust. Bake until the center is firm and the filling does not jiggle when lightly shaken, about 35 minutes.

Serve with fresh berries.

ELIZABETH BEIER
Book Editor

Though we pride ourselves on having been a separate country at one point, Texas has a great tradition of Southern foods like fiery hot grits and fried chicken. Fried chicken was not part of what was on my mother's table *at all*. So when I was about sixteen years old, I wormed out my grandmother's recipe for fried chicken from my mother's sister. There are many different fried chicken theories, but my grandmother's was hot sauce in the milk, and soak overnight in the fridge. I made this for various boyfriends over the years, and it was always a hit. You use a big cauldron of boiling oil to cook it, so there's also a fun, dangerous element to making it.

Everything about my grandmother's cooking was different from my mother's—even the way she put food on the plate was different, and she used different pots and pans. My mother was always, always, *always* an extremely bland cook. She never used garlic; the risk of having bad breath was so great she would never chance it. She had a total horror of spicy things. A horror of vinaigrette because, on a lunch date, it could make you sneezy, and that would be so undignified. In more recent years, at Thanksgiving, my mother would come into my kitchen and try to persuade me to keep spice—and by "spice" I mean garlic, shallots, thyme, salt, sage, nothing that any human being would consider spicy—out of the turkey stuffing. She would say, "People won't tell you this, but they really don't like it." What she perceived as being too intense was actually barely flavored. Since she died, I've been using really spicy andouille sausage in my stuffing.

When I was a little kid, someone gave my mother a fabulous spice rack, with every spice under the sun, and she was so uninterested in it that she let me have it as a toy. I liked to open the bottles and smell the spices and touch them and mix them into different piles. They sat in the kitchen for years, becoming desiccated and horrible, but for a really long time I thought they were fun to play with.

My mom was a terrible cook to begin with, but she also made "healthy" food, which added an additional layer of badness. She had no artistry; she would serve un-adorned tofu, or a piece of white fish that she had oiled and baked in the oven for hours. She bought a juicer very early in the '60s, and we drank a lot of carrot juice with brewer's yeast for breakfast. The minute I could get away, the minute I could drive, I'd go out and get whatever I could to eat. I'd eat with friends—friends always had much more interesting things in their refrigerators—or I'd get barbecue (Texas barbecue is brisket with a tomato-based sauce with honey or molasses in it), or Mexican food, or Tex-Mex. Growing up in Texas, I could always get great trash food; and because the whole state is basically suburban, you can pull over to the side of any road and pick something up. Unbelievable hamburgers. Fabulous fried chicken, of course. And then there are the things you love growing up that are just pure delight. For me, these were corn dogs and Slurpees at 7-Eleven; and Dairy Queen dip cones. There are different versions of the dip cone, but mine was vanilla soft-serve ice cream dipped into chocolate. I didn't feel like I wanted to be somewhere cooking French food; I just wanted something to eat.

There's a place in Fort Worth called Joe T. Garcia's, which has incredibly cheap, wonderful, greasy Mexican food. It's been around forever, and it's a real institution. My mother, when she was a little girl, used to go there and bring decks of cards and reading materials because they won't start cooking anything until you arrive; you could be there all afternoon waiting for them to cook and refry the beans for dinner. I took my daughter to my twenty-fifth high school reunion. Even though we were about to go to a football game with a barbecue, I had to take her to Joe T. Garcia's. We stopped on the way from the airport. There was a big line, one Friday night. I don't know if the guy remembered me or not, but he scooted us right to the front. We had a fabulous meal. You say you want a complete dinner and they bring you nachos with chopped jalapeños, salsa and chips, warm tortillas with butter. Then you have cheese enchiladas, which come with refried beans, a side of guacamole, and two greasy, delicious little beef tacos. All served family style, and you should have a margarita with it. That kind of food doesn't travel well, but barbecue you can stick in your freezer. I told everybody I was bringing back barbecue, and we'd have it when I got home. I brought a cooler and ice packs. I haven't lived in Texas for so long I forgot Angelo's was closed on Sunday.

I have a smell memory of bacon being sizzled in my house, which my mother decided when I was very young was perfectly horrible for you. We never had it again. She was so doctrinaire about that sort of stuff. When we were out shopping, when she wasn't looking I'd run to the front of the grocery store so I could eat a candy bar. We never baked cookies, ever, ever. The closest we came was an okay muffin recipe that had a lot of wheat germ in it, and safflower oil instead of butter, sweetened with honey. My father owned big commercial bakeries in Illinois—not huge bakeries like Pepperidge Farm, but they provided the local sliced white and whole wheat bread. I remember eating something my father brought home from the bakery when I was very little and my mother saying, "Don't feed her that, it's junk! It's made of white flour and it's not doing anything for her body." And my father said, "She's the daughter of a baker; I think she can have some white bread and it's not going to kill her." My mother's philosophy on food was very thought-through, and it was not about enjoyment. In fact, she used to denigrate her sister, who was a reasonably good cook, by saying, "The way you pick your food is based on taste, but that's ridiculous. You should select food because you want to do something positive for your body."

My mother was very censorious of my aunt, who lived on coffee, desserts, steaks, fatty things, and fried things. She thought that was so shortsighted and foolish and animalistic and unrefined. But I would say that in addition to finding things that are good for your body, you should also find things that taste good. There is a happy medium.

I don't think my mother really enjoyed food, although she did think certain things were yummy. She loved ice cream, but she would never eat it. She would say, "I remember once when I was traveling with your father in Egypt, I could not find anything to eat that met my standards. By the end of the second day, when I realized I hadn't had anything to eat, I broke down and bought an ice cream from a vendor." She denied herself, and she really took pleasure in that.

People favor one sense or another. There are certain people who favor taste and they just want to eat delicious things. That wasn't my mother. However, even though she couldn't cook, she did think food was very important. She wasn't afraid of unusual ingredients, or of cooking with food that was very close to its elemental state. I think there's a similarity in that to the sensibility of a cook who actually enjoys it. There are people who don't like to cook who will hold up a turnip and say, "What am I supposed to do with this?" But if you like to cook you say, "Oh well, there are all kinds of things I can do with it." You're ready to get a hold of it and you're not afraid of it; you like it, in fact. Only, as I've said, in my mother's case the idea of eating for pleasure was very, very foreign. My father and I used to bond over that. Dinner would have been so horrible, we'd be so hungry, and we'd run into each other at the refrigerator late at night: "Is there anything in there we can make a sandwich out of?" Because we were starving.

My mother traveled a lot and had a bad case of Anglophilia and Francophilia. Being a bad cook to begin with, combined with the health food, and combined with her love of French and English ingredients, meant that her meal choices never meshed properly. For lunch, she would pack me—and think about how embarrassing this is when you're in the first or second grade—whole-grain bread with a tin of imported foie gras, and a clementine, and a triangle of Laughing Cow cheese. I was mortified; I used to throw my lunch in the bushes. I would cadge a Twinkie from someone at school and spend my allowance money on baloney and cheese on white bread with yellow mustard, or eat a cafeteria burger. No one would ever have traded lunches with me.

But one fun thing my mother always did when she traveled was spend a lot of time shopping in grocery stores, poking around for things to bring home. She loved figuring out what people's daily lives were about, and a way to do that was to see what they bought. One of the things she got on her travels, which is now a little easier to find than it used to be, was canned *ventresca*, or belly tuna. I remember her ordering a case of it. I made a couple of good dishes out of that tuna back at home that I still make from time to time, like linguine with *ventresca:* warm a can of ventresca with garlic, then toss it with cooked linguine and kosher salt and a big handful of minced Italian parsley.

Mostly, though, my mother was into packaging. She liked triangular milk cartons, and how yogurt in different countries comes in differently shaped containers, and weirdly shaped sugar cubes. She would buy upscale convenience food, because she wouldn't be planning to cook with it. I, on the other hand, would be shopping along with her, buying branch spices, and hot sauces, and pepper mixtures— *ingredients*—wondering, worrying, "Are we allowed to bring this back?" I still do that; I'll go to France on vacation and come back with a pound of salt in my bag.

My parents and I would go over to Europe in the summer on the *QE2*, and on other ships, too. I remember an Italian ship called the *Michelangelo*, and eating the children's meals on board. They were so delicious—pasta that wasn't overcooked, with a tomato Bolognese sauce. There was nothing fancy about the food; it was prepared quickly for little kids. I don't think gravity is the right word to describe those ship dinners, but there was a certain way you were meant to eat a meal, there was a certain cadence to it, and each meal had several courses: a pasta course, and then a meat or fish course, and then there was a pause, and then there was dessert. I guess I would also say there was a stateliness to eating this way, even at a long table with a bunch of noisy kids. And I thought, "Well, this is fun, this is *great*. It's like having a tea party every night." In our house at dinner, there weren't courses, there wouldn't be dessert, there would be everything on the table at once—the salad and the fruit and a main dish—and then as soon as we were finished eating, we'd fly up and run off.

My parents and I also spent a lot of time in Mexico, which is essentially in the backyard of Texas. It was wild but tame. It was exotic but nearby. At the time, my mother was learning to speak Spanglish, and that was another part of her interest. Plus it was really cheap. You could do a lot in Mexico, and stay there for a long time, with a lot of people helping you, for not very much money. I remember loving that I was allowed—and I don't know why I was allowed—to wander around Mexico City by myself when I was ten, eleven, twelve years old. I would start in the morning by going to the hotel restaurant and ordering huevos rancheros. In Texas, you can't get around when you're a kid; someone has to drive you everywhere because you can't walk and there's no public transportation. But in Mexico City, after breakfast, I would trot around the city completely on my own. There were wonderful *pastelerías*, or pastry shops, there. I adored the Ideal. It was big, bustling, exciting. I don't remember that there was anything so unusual to eat there—big buns with different-colored hard sugar on top, and raisins; they weren't that delicious and a lot of them tasted the same and were kind of bland—but I loved the way you took a tray, and tongs, and went around choosing your own pastries. And I appreciated that the Ideal had beautiful bakery boxes: blue and pink with fabulous filigree designs on them. I would fill one of those up, take it back to the hotel, and work through the pastries over the weekend.

In fairness, my mother did make a few things well, which were inspired by her travels. I believe one of them is her own creation. Part of her Anglophilia was a love of precious, tea sandwich-y things. She used to make a great sandwich of shredded carrots and grated Monterey Jack cheese on raisin bread with mayonnaise. It's absolutely delightful. She made a great chicken and chutney sandwich. But she didn't own a real knife. How can you cook without a knife? I'd try to bring knives into the home so that we would be able to chop things. And she would say, "Oh we don't need that. If we want to chop anything, we have this paring knife."

I believe my own kids should be able to make things. They should be able to figure out that they can do stuff. The kitchen is one of the easiest places to start. They can figure out that making something to eat doesn't take that long, that they can assemble ingredients and do this or that with them. I hate when they whine and cry because something isn't happening. Do you remember Romper Room? And the Think and Do Girl? "We have a problem, but what can we do to solve it?" My two-year-old son sits there and says, "I'm hungry, I want to have . . ." And you *can* have it if you go in and get some tools and fire up the stove.

I like the work of the kitchen. I walk in the door at seven P.M. after a day at the office and I'm dying to be with my kids, but I'm also dying to start making dinner. So everyone comes into the kitchen with me. They sit on the floor playing and watching what's going on. It's kind of fun in there—the kitchen has knobs and dials and gadgets, and measuring. It offers a great sense of accomplishment—that's one reason I like to cook. It doesn't require a huge amount of time, or effort, or funds, or anything, and you get a tangible and necessary thing at the end of the process.

I especially love project cooking. I love to make puff pastry, which is a real two-day project. I take great pleasure in buying a cheap cut of meat and figuring out how to make it delicious. Western Beef (a New York City chain of budget meat stores) is my dream come true. If I were actually organized enough to buy a whole week's worth of groceries at a time, I could feed our entire family for a hundred bucks, I think, with great, lavish, perfect dishes. I love capturing the greenmarket between my daughter's school and the office. I show up with a chicken in my purse and have to figure out how to keep it cold for the day. Something in me wants to feed everyone for a hundred dollars, and to live in this sort of French fashion, picking up perfect little ingredients for the night as I go. No matter what I do for a living, what I'm really doing is composing my grocery list.

It's so great to make something delicious out of something that could almost be considered garbage. Not offal, because no one in my house will eat that. But veal breast, say, which is a very tough, ugly, fatty cut of meat. If you treat it right, with a big marination, then a sauté of something, and then a long cook in the oven, with the application of a little bit of time and a little bit of effort you can transform it. A breast of veal could feed eight people for four dollars. You either have time or money.

You can always serve people fabulous lamb chops and caviar for a lot of money and no time. Or you can take a lot of time and make a veal breast.

Occasionally, I fall for a gadget, which I stay interested in for a while and then put away and never look at again. I recently fell for a slow cooker. My interest is still going strong, but it's seasonal, and I'm about to put the pot away for the summer. The slow cooker is not perfect at all, but it's very useful if you're a person who works. You can make a real dish by just time-shifting your efforts to ten at night. The process of cooking with a slow cooker (which is a classier way of referring to a Crock-Pot) is closely related to the pleasures of a good stew. Some time and the application of a minimal amount of effort can turn humble ingredients (and, yes, cheap cuts of meat) into something so warm and fragrant. It's also a way for me to cook during the week the way I like to cook on weekends. If I open up my slow cooker and throw in a veal breast, some sliced leeks, some sage, minced shallots, salt, and a bit of liquid right before bed and turn on the pot, I wake up to the most delectable smells. Then, as a practical matter, the stew or meat can rest all day in the fridge, and dinner is essentially ready the minute I walk in the door.

I remember going to someone's house for dinner ten years ago, and I knew as I was eating that I recognized the food from somewhere. Suddenly I realized, Oh my God, this is an entire dinner from the International Poultry Company. It was pretty good: rotisserie chicken and mashed potatoes. But these people had invited us to dinner and hadn't even made dinner. There wasn't any compelling reason why they couldn't have. I said, "That was delicious," and then I thought later in the meal, Wasn't that her moment to say "I didn't make it?" I feel on some deep level that it's cheating to bring in that sort of thing, except in an utter pinch. Dinner is about eating exactly what you want, but it's also about *making* something to eat.

I recently threw a book party for Alisa Valdes-Rodriguez and the publication of her first novel, *The Dirty Girls Social Club*. It was so fun planning what the food was going to be and making it. Each of the girls in the novel has a different background; they're all American, but one has Cuban parents, one Colombian, one Puerto Rican, and so forth. And since there are six girls, and six is about the right number of things to pass around at a cocktail party, I made a little nibble from each girl's background. From Miami/Cuba: mini Cuban sandwiches; from Colombia: yucca cakes with *queso fresco* (a fresh white cheese similar to farmer cheese); from Mexico/California: Cal-Mex shrimp with chipotle mayo; from Spain: chorizo rounds with cilantro; from Cuba: *baccala* (codfish) cakes with lime aioli; from Puerto Rico: *surullitos* (cornmeal sticks), both plain and with *picadillo* (a dish of ground meat with tomatoes, garlic, and onions); and as an extra: banana bread with guava butter. I even made the bread for the sandwiches. I could have bought Cuban loaves from an excellent bakery I know of, but I would have felt then as though I hadn't actually made those little *media noches*, just assembled them.

I love to make things, really—books, meals, children. I can't sew for beans, so one of the most productive things I can put time into, project-wise, is recipes. And don't you think you end up feeling like a magician when you turn a little pile of powdery white stuff and water into something as excellent as bread? Sometimes it's almost as much fun to think of a theme and assemble dishes in my head as it is to do the actual cooking and shopping—and that was true for the *Dirty Girls* party.

Cooking is second nature to me. When I came home from the hospital with my daughter, I was pretty uncomfortable because I had had an episiotomy. I was determined to have beef stew, though, and I had my husband bring me the chopping board so I could chop things while I sat in the couch. I think the need for stew was probably more about something I felt regarding parenthood than it was about cooking and food. I felt very strongly that it was a beef stew day, the first stew day of fall (my daughter, Anna, was born September 25), and my making it as I normally would have was an acknowledgment that life was better but not different with a child; that the little baby would integrate into our fairly well established routines and lives. I had just turned thirty-seven, so although having her was just the best and most important thing ever, I knew it didn't mean that the rest of what I liked and did (work, reading, cooking, my friendships) was going to go away. Even if unstated, I think that's a big fear with first children—you know, the moan of, "Now we're a boring old couple with children, and it's got to be all about the kid." I knew right away that wasn't going to be true for us. That we could, in Helen Gurley Brown's phrase, have it all.

As I was breastfeeding my daughter, I wondered, "Could I make breast milk ice cream?" That sprang from the great pleasure I take in the idea of "living off the land": What can we make? How can we use something three ways? That kind of thing. There's nothing better in summer than to be able to make dinner completely from the garden, with maybe some pasta thrown in, or arborio for a pea risotto. One night while I was pumping and storing, I saw the cream that had risen to the top of the already-refrigerated bottle of breast milk and thought: "Hmm, bet that would work in an ice cream maker. Using all the milk would be too watery, but if you just skimmed the cream and sweetened it. . . ." But I never did try it because the milk was too precious for recipe experimentation.

• MY GRANDMOTHER RUBY'S FRIED CHICKEN •

Serves 4

1½ quarts buttermilk

1 tray ice cubes

¼ cup coarse salt, plus more for seasoning the flour

6 to 8 generous lashings of Tabasco or
other red hot sauce

1 fryer chicken, rinsed well and dried,
cut into 8 pieces

1 (16 ounce) can Crisco (or one and one-half cans,
depending on the size of your skillet)

2 eggs, beaten

1 dinner plate's worth all-purpose flour

Black pepper (not freshly ground,
but from a little red McCormick box)

Put the buttermilk in a large pitcher with the ice cubes. Shake or stir for a minute or two until it is as cold as it can be, then strain and discard the ice cubes. Add the salt and Tabasco to buttermilk and stir until well blended. Pour into one or two large Ziploc bags with the chicken pieces and refrigerate overnight, or for at least 4 hours. Remove the chicken and drain on paper towels, patting skin dry.

In an old, deep, cast iron skillet heat the Crisco on medium-high heat until melted and beginning to shimmer (you can also use vegetable oil or Mazola for frying, but it's not as good as Crisco). The melted fat should come a bit more than halfway up the side of your pan.

Put the egg in a medium bowl. Put the flour on a plate and doctor with the pepper and more salt. Dredge the chicken pieces in the egg and then in the flour.

Fry the white pieces of chicken together first and the dark ones together second. Leave the chicken pieces in the fat long enough before turning so that the first sides are a deep golden brown, 10 to 15 minutes. Then turn and fry the second sides (this will take about half the time it took to fry the first side).

Do not cover the skillet, but let yourself and your stove and your wall become festively dappled with bits of atomized Crisco.

Remove the chicken from the fat and drain on brown paper bags. Serve at once, hot, or let it come to room temperature and take it on a picnic with a big tub of coleslaw and some fresh biscuits made with Lily self-rising flour and drizzled with honey when they come out of the oven.

• FIERY GRITS •

Serves 4

2 cups hominy grits
Salt
½ pound Monterey Jack cheese, grated
½ cup butter
2 teaspoons Tabasco
2 cloves garlic, minced
3 eggs, beaten
2 green chilies (from a can, or dried and plumped up
with water), chopped
2 jalepeño peppers, fresh or canned,
seeded and chopped

In a medium saucepan, heat 4 cups of salted water to boiling over high heat. Add grits, stirring to keep the grits from clumping. Lower heat and simmer grits, stirring constantly until they start pulling away from the sides of the pan.

Preheat oven to 350°F and butter a 2-quart baking dish.

Add cheese, butter, Tabasco, garlic, eggs, chilies, and jalepeños to the grits and stir well. Mix in other ingredients.

Bake for 45 minutes until golden on top.

Serve hot.

• CROCK-POT DUCK •

This recipe is about the best thing I've ever made. Veal breast can be substituted for duck. In that instance, use white wine or beer instead of red wine (this is not so much a taste issue, but red wine makes veal an unappetizing muddy lavender color); make sure to sear the breast on the fatty side first in the sauté pan; stud the breast with cloves rather than scattering them in the slow cooker; and omit the broiling step after the breast comes out of the slow cooker.

Serves 4

1 (5 to 6 pound) duck, fresh or completely thawed if frozen, quartered and fat removed

Freshly ground black pepper

Kosher salt

2 ribs celery, chopped

2 medium carrots, peeled and sliced

½ large white or Spanish onion, peeled and sliced

2 shallots, peeled and diced

1 large sprig thyme, on the branch

6 whole cloves

8 whole peppercorns

¼ cup good red wine

Juice of ½ lemon

Heat a large sauté pan over medium-high heat for 3 to 5 minutes. Add the duck and brown well, skin side first, then flesh side, about 15 minutes altogether.

Lift the duck from the pan. Pepper and liberally salt it on both sides and set aside.

In the slow cooker, mix celery, carrots, onion, shallots, thyme, cloves, peppercorns, and red wine. Place the duck on top of this mixture, skin side up. Pour the lemon juice over the duck and sprinkle on a bit more kosher salt.

Slow cook the duck on low for 8 to 10 hours.

Drain the liquid from the slow cooker (this can be strained, chilled, and saved in a bowl—it will separate when cooled into perfect duck fat on the top and lovely duck gelée on the bottom).

After this step, duck can be refrigerated, covered, up to two days, before proceeding.

Set oven to broil. Put duck in a broiling pan and broil, skin side up only, until skin is completely crisp, about 3 to 5 minutes.

Serve on a bed of vegetables from the slow cooker, picking out the cloves, peppercorns, and thyme branch. I usually pick out the carrot slices from the vegetables, scatter them on the plate, and discard the rest.

CHARLOTTE GOULD

Founder, Not-for-Profit Organization
Mothers Across America (MAAM)

Everything in my entire food culture is French. I was born in Geneva, where my parents both worked for the United Nations; then we moved across the border to a small French town in Normandy. Until I was five years old, I had the incredible privilege of living on a farm where they were making crème fraîche down the road. One of my earliest memories is a whole herd of cows getting in through the gates of our farm and tramping over the flowers. I remember going into stores and seeing big vats of crème fraîche and bottles of Calvados—things that were very typical of that area, which was close to Normandy. And I remember the intense smell of cheese, of being overcome by dairy. We used to keep our Camembert and Epoisses outside in the summertime, and I remember my brother crying because he couldn't stand the smell of those incredibly pungent cheeses.

After France, my family moved to Washington, D.C.; then we spent all our long summers returning to Europe. My mother always had to be somewhere near the water for her sanity. If we weren't right on the coast we'd be up in the Alpes Maritime in some lovely sixteenth-century place, from where we'd have a hair-raising ride down to the beach. One of my first important and substantial food memories is eating fresh fruit that we bought in Nice. I was pretty young. I couldn't identify my appreciation at that age, but the peach was the size of a melon and dripping, and I'd never had anything like it. The figs were the same, practically the size of emu eggs, huge and pink, and I had never had a fig before. And raspberries were the size of golf balls. I just gorged.

I have strong memories of my mother cooking all throughout my childhood. I remember her peeling grapes for me, which is something very erotic for a mother to do for her daughter. I remember sitting at the dinner table and, even in bad family circumstances, the food was always great, and it was always the focus of our lives. My mother went to extraordinary lengths to make wonderful meals every night. She loved to cook, and it was her way of channeling something for all of us to enjoy into the family. I think it was her one way of holding us together. She and my father had an unhappy marriage, so even though there was love going into the food . . . Well, would you cook for someone you hated and enjoy it?

My mother would make things that were so sophisticated. For my fifth birthday, she made one of Julia Child's famous brandy cakes, which she soaked for five days. It didn't occur to her that she was feeding a bunch of five-year-olds. Parents came to pick up their kids, who were sick everywhere, reeking of booze. I once poured a whole vat of strawberry soup down the toilet—this was strawberry with chicken stock and tarragon, nothing sweet that a child might enjoy. My brother and I were never treated like children. Because we were accustomed to having glamorous dinners every night that we had to get dressed up for, when we had dinner parties and there were other kids around, we were thrilled to get hot dogs.

When she threw dinner parties, my mother would always have me help clearing, and I would always catch somebody licking the plates. Specifically, one of our neighbors, who was a very uptight, upper-crust antiques dealer. My mother used to make an oyster and artichoke gratin. I walked into the dining room one night after she'd served this dish and saw the antiques dealer picking up everybody else's plate and licking it. That really made an impression on me. Cooking in my mother's house wasn't some intangible thing. Food was equal to social life. It felt important. At Thanksgiving, my mother would ask every stray person to dinner; to me, that's what Thanksgiving is about—about family, yes, but also about reaching out to people who have nowhere else to go. I remember having to sit next to my fifth-grade geometry teacher, thinking, Why did she have to invite *him*?

My mother worked for a while as the food editor of a cookbook series. She hates these books with a passion. I think she considers them kind of provincial, and loathes the American food mentality, which is so evident to her in the books—a penchant for food that is flashy and unsophisticated; quantity over quality; sugar added to every vinaigrette. She also felt cheated out of her own contribution to the books because they had to be so formulaic. But her hand is in a lot of those recipes. She was assigned to devise some recipes for *Snacks and Sandwiches*. It was a funny outlet for her—sandwiches are *not* her thing. So she built this incredibly complex sandwich, which is on the cover of one of the books. The formal description of it from the inside page reads: "A composite loaf formed from layers of diverse ingredients yields a vividly patterned slice. To create the cross-sectional geometry, a whole sandwich loaf was sliced horizontally, then bound together by wine-flavored butter [my mother put alcohol in every possible thing] studded with pistachios, parboiled asparagus, strips of ham, and baked mushroom caps." I remember eating test versions, and how friends would look at me in disbelief and disgust at school when I pulled my "sandwich" out of a brown paper bag. She also developed a recipe for another book in the series that has become nationally famous: chopped egg and cream cheese and scallion and cheap caviar that are layered in a pie pan. I see this at parties everywhere.

My mother had an amazing cookbook collection, which is the foundation of mine, because she gave it to me. When I moved to Whistler, British Columbia, for a year, after I met my husband, Ross, even though I knew I was only going to be out there temporarily, I sent all my pots—about a hundred pounds of copper, most of it turn-of-the-century, which my mother purchased at a château estate sale in France—

and my entire cookbook collection. I have a sentimental attachment to the books. Often, when I'm feeling stressed, I will flip through one or two I haven't looked at in a long time to remind myself of the possibilities of cooking, to feel calm, to feel a little more educated. I suppose I was taking with me to Whistler the things that were closest to my heart and which defined me. I couldn't—I can't—imagine not having them around.

Food connects me to the world in a very automatic way. Everywhere in the world I go, I'll walk into any food store to browse. I'll stop at every restaurant I haven't seen before to look at the menu. I don't have to worry on my way home about picking something up for dinner. I know that nothing is going to prevent me from doing that; I'm not going to forget. I hope my four-year-old daughter, India, takes away the same joy from cooking and food, and also comes to see meals as important social and family events.

Ross and I took India to San Sebastian, Spain, when she was a year old. She ate gobs and gobs of anchovies on that trip, and Serrano ham, and cows lips risotto. And I thought, *That* is my daughter, no question. It was a very satisfying experience. I hope food will bring her happy memories. Now we're screaming at her to eat her food, because she's in her "white" phase, and I'm thinking, Let's not do this. Still, if I give her something left over, she'll turn around and say, "No, that's from yesterday, I want something fresh." Or, "You put too much rosemary in this." It's ridiculous. But it's also very funny. I feel proud that she can tell good produce from bad, recognize herbs, set standards, be critical of what she eats, though it makes my life harder at the moment.

India can peel garlic and crush it; she can peel cucumbers and scoop out seeds. She loves marinating meats and oiling the pans. The first thing she ever wanted to do in the kitchen was mix vinaigrettes. She's desperate to do it every night. I don't know if my mother consciously decided to give me the gift of loving to cook, but she did, and it's something I absolutely want to pass on to my own daughter.

Cooking can be therapeutic and very private, and there are times when I don't want anyone in my kitchen. Because we live in an open space, the kitchen counter is really the hub; the mail goes on it, everything that's current goes on it. I put India up there from the time she was really young. She likes to sit on the counter, and sometimes I just want Ross to get her off—take her away! This is sometimes due to impatience on my part, which I feel when India tips things over, or insists on whisking or folding too hard. I feel terrible when I get impatient with her, but the truth is, when I'm in the kitchen, I usually prefer to be alone. I am claustrophobic; this may be part of it. But I think I'm also protective of my territory. As a mother, you sacrifice everything; it's so important to find the simple things in life that can make you happy on a daily basis. For me, this is preparing food alone, in peace.

I can't separate cooking from my own identity. Identity is a funny word, because it's a conscious word. But certainly anyone who knows me would say that it's the first thing on my list. Everything I remember growing up that was emotional, good or bad, happened around the dinner table. It's hard not to relate my draw to cooking at least in part to the negative atmosphere in my parents' home. The kitchen was always a very safe place. With all the tension in the house, my mother and I could be in there with our individual duties and just go at it. Even though I know my mother was resentful to have to cook for my father, she managed to change that bad energy into dynamic energy. I inherited this escape-route habit from her. When I am frustrated, stressed, feeling sad, I often relegate myself to the kitchen because I know I can be productive there and that it will make me feel better.

Food is a completely natural part of my life, and that was how I landed in the food business after college. It had nothing to do with wanting to go into the food business; it was really a matter of survival. I only enjoyed the first couple years of it, and that was because it was novel, and I was twenty-three years old when I started my business, and I had so much to learn about life. I was going to be a sculptor. I was working for a sculptor who was successful enough to hire a caterer, and I thought cooking would be a good way to supplement my income as an artist. Sotheby's auction house eventually came to me, and I opened a café for them, which I ran for ten years. Skinny Lunch developed from feeding these incredibly weight-conscious women at Sotheby's, and it was the first-ever lunch delivery service. I built up four thousand clients in three years. I was so burned out and so miserable, and I didn't even have the opportunity to share any of my cooking skills. When you're working in the catering business, you're mass-producing food. People want what they want—

it's not about you. It's not creative. I'm so thrilled now to have no connection between cooking a meal and thinking about what's going on in my professional kitchen.

Still, the only time I was turned off food was after Ross's fortieth birthday party. I really pushed myself to go over the top for that event. I threw a sit-down dinner for forty-seven people, eight courses, many of which had multiple components. This was the menu, including wines that Ross's brother chose to accompany the food:

- Tuna, coconut and lime cake (*Cava Brut, Oriol Rossell, Cava, Spain*)

- A trio of soups: mushroom with pear and cumin, coconut with rosemary oil and parmesan crisp, pumpkin with Tomme de Savoie and hazelnut veil (*1999 Riesling, Familie Molitor, Mosel-Saar-Ruwer, Germany*)

- Foie gras sandwich with sesame salt, apricot-bean purée, and sweet-and-sour reduction (*2001 Scheurebe Kabinett "Munsterer Dautenpflanzer" Ohler'sches, Rheinhessen, Germany*)

- Salmon two ways: cured and seared with pine needles; confit with balsamic and baby arugula

- Halibut fillet on a sweet onion tart with an éclat of olive oil and tomato conserve (*Botromagno 2001 Gravina, Apulia, Italy*)

- Venison tenderloin with a lemon squash purée, turnip gratin, apple cake, and juniper berry juice (*2000 Domaine du Fraisse, Faugers, France*)

- Warm quince soup

- Two cheeses: warm Maroilles with cashew cream and yogurt sauce; goat cheese torte with figs, pine nuts, and mint

- Panna cotta with Sauternes jelly; chocolates with lavender, rosemary, violet, and black olive (*Muscat, Samos Union des Cooperatives Vinicoles de Samos, Greece*)

It had to be a big deal—so many of our friends were traveling long distances to attend. And since Ross doesn't like anything subtle, I knew I had to find exotic ingredients. One of Ross's friends was flying in from Seattle, and I had him go out and chop some Douglas fir for me to wrap the salmon in. Throwing the party was fun. I could justify spending *x* amount of money when we hadn't been able to entertain in a long time the way we'd like to because we couldn't afford it. I'd just been on a trip to Provençe so I was feeling inspired by Provençal food—the thyme, lavender, rosemary, olive oil. I worked for two weeks, ten-hour days, with my mother. As payback for having to chop onions and wash greens for her years ago, I relished the opportunity to have her prep for me. The fights were unreal. The potato leaves for the foie gras sandwiches took almost a whole day between the two of us. I had to borrow my neighbor's oven; we were running up and down the stairs with red-hot baking sheets, swearing, sweating, and in the end we only got a ten-percent return. Sometimes my mother would come up with a batch, and I'd tell her they were too dark, and she'd say, "Do it yourself." This went on all day. Then she'd eat one of the perfectly golden ones instead of one of the burned ones, and I would scream because it meant another hour of work just to reproduce that one.

Another classic moment was making my mother finely hand grate three hundred hazelnuts. I wouldn't let her put them through a Cuisinart or chop them with a knife because they would have lost all their delicious oils. It was a truly cruel job; the only worse job I can think of is when I had to stuff three hundred *chilies relleños* and then deep fry them when I worked for a caterer in Seattle. I can't even remember which plate the hazelnuts were for, but they tragically never made it to the table, as we discovered the next day. Boy did we have a good laugh about that . . . in the end. Not at first, though. It was just inconceivable that those hours of toil were for naught.

A good environment for cooking is one that's relaxed, although when I cook, even though I love it, I get in the worst possible moods. It always turns into screaming and throwing things. There is always an element of stress. It is funny thinking about why I do something that can cause me so much grief. I'm probably a perfectionist, and cooking is in the details. One Christmas, when I had my family and my boyfriend's family for dinner, my brother accidentally threw my precious goose fat for cooking the venison down the drain. I made him go to the Food Emporium, get a duck, and skin it, and everyone had to wait an hour in between courses.

I hardly ever sit down to a meal I've cooked and feel good about it. I may think, Yeah, it's okay. And that's part of being a cook—the process sort of ruins your ability to taste. Or maybe you build up a tolerance to it. If I'm trying to perfect a particular flavor, trying to get it just right, I sit down to serve it and to me it tastes flat. Especially coming from French cooking, which is bursting with flavor. Sometimes I surprise myself. I sit down and think, That tastes pretty good. I know this is hard for people in my family, and I don't do it to fish for attention, but I will often put something down and say, "This didn't work out," or "This could have been so much better," or "God, I'm so sorry, I totally overcooked the lentils." I think I have a right to say it—it's just an honest feeling that needs to be expressed, and a cook is her own best critic. The most disgusting thing I ever made was a frittata for Christmas breakfast. I don't know what I was thinking, but I cooked it in a cast-iron pan for an hour. It came out like meringue. I took one bite and then I went to everyone's plate and took it off with my hands. I'm not a negative person at all, and these failures don't take my joy out of it, so I guess what I love about cooking is that it is a process.

I think the movie *Babette's Feast*, which is about a French chef who escapes civil unrest in France and moves to an austere and religious town in Jutland, Denmark, resonated deeply for many cooks. I can see myself doing what Babette eventually does in the movie: using all my money to make one great meal. Cooking is so much about the moment—an endless moment—and that moment is everything. I'm not sure if people who don't cook can appreciate the complete and utter submission to building the perfect meal at all costs. It's a wonderful feeling to do that, even if you think nothing turned out exactly the way you wanted it to. There's a scene in the movie in which Babette is standing out in the freezing weather with ocean water lapping over her skirts, waiting for the arrival of a sea turtle and other goods she's ordered from France. I could feel her anticipation and joy to have these things arriving, of having them all there. Later, halfway through dinner, you see this incredible transformation of the guests, who have vowed not to enjoy the meal, as they wonder, How could food be this good? That's when everything turns around and they all become deeply committed to the meal. There was the feeling at that moment that it was going to last forever.

I can relate to burrowing myself away and not thinking about anything else. Generally speaking, I never feel like I have enough time to do anything, but I can always find the time to throw a dinner party. For that, I can put everything else out of my mind. I'm a distance runner, and through my organization, Mothers Across America (MAAM), which attempts to empower mothers through sports, I teach running as a meditative sport, and when I run, I can succeed at just thinking about breathing. I suppose I have an obsession with the body, and the way that food nurtures the body and soul, so do sports. Both running and cooking are wholly satisfying, challenging, require concentration, and have the power to sweep you off your feet. Cooking for others and contributing to the lives of mothers through MAAM are all about giving, sharing—what I like to do best.

I also relate to Babette's quest for the perfect materials. With certain chefs, like Paula Wolfert and Charlie Trotter, there can be no substitutions. I will ship stuff in at great expense to get just the right thing, even if I can't afford it. I once was trying to find *verjus*—which is a sort of a vinegar made with grapes picked very green so that the acidity is low—for Charlie Trotter's Mushroom Soup with Pear Relish and Cumin Oil. I put everybody through hell, namely Ross, who always has to run around shopping for my dinner parties. He'd call me up and say, "Well, I can't find it, can we use something else?"

"No!" He knows the answer—why even ask? As a feminist, it's a great feeling to take what is traditionally viewed as a menial and subservient chore, flip it around, turn it into an art form, derive pleasure from it while gaining control over central household territory—putting the ball in the cook's court, I guess.

Eating well is satisfying—and by "eating well," I mean having a proper meal and sitting down to eat something that's complete rather than having a sandwich. A perfect meal for me includes fresh, high-quality ingredients; a wine that marries with the food; friends; a simple table; dogs at my feet; maybe a foie gras and Sauternes to start; duck à l'orange or a melt-in-your-mouth fish; a plate of French vegetables; cheese with Comice pears. I think it's sad that so many people don't know how to cook, or how to tell whether food is fresh, or ripe. Not being able to distinguish good food is like being color-blind; you can't appreciate all the subtle differences in taste and flavor. More than it is a way to provide something basic, cooking is a structure around which I build my day, a skeleton of life.

PAM GOULD

Charlotte's mother recalls preparations for
Ross's fortieth birthday party

Last November, my son-in-law turned forty. His wife, my daughter, decided to commemorate this event by throwing a dinner party for forty some odd of his widely scattered friends—a seated dinner with eight courses and serious wines. I got the call to set aside the week immediately preceding the birthday and travel to New York to help prep for it. I love my daughter. Our underlying mutual regard, however, has suffered a possibly irreversible setback as a consequence of that week and, although the bleeding has stopped, months later I am still unwilling to peel an onion or spend more than five minutes on the preparation of a meal.

Arriving after a 350-mile drive, brain-dead and exhausted, I expected a reclining chair, a generous glass of iced Riesling, and a tumultuous welcome. Instead, I got some no-name wine slopped into a beer glass, some crackers and tuna, and was told to get on with it; the birthday boy was out for the evening, and as the whole party was to be a surprise, we needed to use every free minute to make a good head start. My head spun. I tried dully to conceive of how to keep secret the arrival of forty international guests and the storage of rented tables, chairs, linens, silver- and stemware, shipments of chocolates from France, rare palm leaves from California, crates of fruit, fish, meat, fowl from local markets, and my own unexplained visit. I was informed that we would begin prepping as soon as Ross left for work in the morning, but that all evidence must be cleared away before he returned in the evening, and we were to appear relaxed and dressed for dinner when he came home. Food was to be stored in the lofts of neighboring artists, all of whom had generously offered their refrigerators. Guests and purveyors were instructed to send delivery and travel plans by FedEx so that the honoree could not accidentally pick up a telephone message. My darling granddaughter was threatened with permanent disablement if she breathed a word, and her nanny was instructed to keep her charge in the park unless there was an ice storm, in which case she was to be taken to a friend's house until she was so tired that she could be brought home, bathed, fed, and put to bed. After the first day, my daughter and I, at daggers drawn, barely spoke.

My first duty of that dreadful week was to peel and mince 190 cloves of garlic. That was the high point. After that came six hundred hazelnuts to be peeled and finely grated, meats to be prepared and marinades made, an exotic aquarium to be deboned and filleted or stuffed and wrapped in those rare palm leaves from California, emulsions to be created and butters flavored. Everything my daughter did was perfect; everything I did was in direct contravention of her explicit instructions. My nut chopping would ruin the party. I had not melted the chocolate correctly. It was the wrong chocolate. Didn't I know how to get the essence from a beet, to clarify butter, to prepare tomato diamonds, to make a pea-shoot coulis or an orange confit? Did she have to explain everything? How had I got through the rest of my life? Could I manage some potatoes?

"Yes," I said. I was given two hundred potatoes and a mandoline and told to produce paper-thin slices trimmed exactly to the same size to be used, when baked, to make foie gras sandwiches. This may sound simple, but a mandoline is lethal when one's fingers are already numb, and my progress was slow and imperfect. Two hundred slices were scornfully swept into the garbage, and hundreds more potatoes appeared. All communication ceased, and in silence I oiled the baking trays and began my lonely trek up and down in the elevator to an absent neighbor's oven.

Unfortunately this oven—had anyone thought to inspect it—would not have passed muster. The temperature soared immediately to five hundred degrees and then dropped to almost zero. The potatoes were either burned black or came out raw. In this way, we rapidly ran out of potatoes. Could I go out and buy more? This purchase required a descent of five floors in the elevator and eight blocks' walk each way. I attracted attention when (a half-hundredweight of potatoes on each arm), I tripped on the gutter and half my potatoes rolled headlong into the oncoming traffic. When the light changed, two Hispanic kids helped me retrieve those that had not been pulverized. Riding the elevator back up, teeth bared, I waited for my daughter to ask me what had taken me so long. But she was crying because her convection oven had burned her hazelnut pavés. I thought of the six hundred nuts I had labored over and wept with her while, in my mind, there irrationally arose a line of poetry from schooldays: "And into the battle rode the six hundred . . .," something to do, I think, with the British Empire in India, taught both as heroic and tragic. Eventually, the pavés were remade and then forgotten by the waiters, who never served them.

In the meantime, my daughter-in-law, also conscripted into service, arrived, having deposited her family in the apartment with the defective oven. The generous owners, having gone to the Caribbean on holiday, lent their apartment on condition that we care for their kitten. In preparation for the party, it was my daughter-in-law's responsibility to count plates, silver, linen, and stemware as the crates arrived, then repack and store them. The magnitude of this job (remember, there were more than forty guests and eight courses) can, without excessive exaggeration, be compared to the pantry of the *Queen Mary II* on its maiden voyage. No two counts were the same. From the kitchen, one could hear my usually quiet and elegant daughter-in-law screaming at the delivery boys, who were dumping crates of wineglasses among those that had been counted and separated. Then the tables and chairs arrived and, with them, an insoluble problem. They did not fit into two very large rooms without the removal of a considerable amount of personal furniture. The neighboring artists were once again appealed to, and all work in the building ceased while furniture was moved up and down the stairs in rehearsal, and plans outlined for the morrow. My daughter left to buy eight dozen red roses while her sister-in-law and I, left to do the cleanup, quietly opened a bottle of rare wine and consumed it, guilt-free.

We pulled it off, of course, as one always does. We arranged the furniture and the lights and the dozens of roses and seated the forty-plus come from all over the world.

We opened wine and placed the marvelous menus about and smiled and were charming. The honoree, when he arrived, *was* surprised.

The next morning, while my grandchildren played in the debris, we had the hazelnut pavés for breakfast.

• FOIE GRAS SANDWICHES WITH APRICOT-BEAN PURÉE, SWEET-AND-SOUR REDUCTION, TOASTED SESAME SEEDS, AND ASSORTED GREENS •

The thing to consider with this dish is whether to make the foie gras from scratch or to purchase a prebaked terrine. You can buy an excellent quality terrine from D'Artagnan, which might save you some headache, but if you're feeling game, follow the instructions below. Baking the foie gras in a green pineapple is very easy and gives a wonderful, subtly tropical flavor. The only real obstacle is cleaning the foie gras well without damaging it.
Adapted from Essential Cuisine *by Michel Bras*

Serves 10

DUCK FOIE GRAS
Adapted from Foie Gras, Magret and Other Good Food from Gascony *by André Daguin and Anne de Ravel*

1 duck foie gras

Fine salt

Freshly ground white pepper

1 unripe pineapple

⅔ cup white rum

Coarse salt

Preheat oven to 200°F.

Clean and devein the foie gras. Season well with fine salt and pepper.

Cut the top off the pineapple, including 2 inches of the body as well as the plume, leaving the pineapple intact. Scoop out the flesh from the body using a sturdy spoon, leaving about an inch-thick wall and taking care not to pierce the skin. Season the cavity of the pineapple with salt and pepper much as you would the cavity of a chicken. Pour in the rum, put the foie gras inside the pineapple, put the top back on, and wrap the whole thing in a generous layer of aluminum foil.

Pour a layer of coarse salt directly onto a baking sheet, which will allow the pineapple to stand securely without wobbling. Bake for 1½ hours, or until the internal temperature of the foie gras reaches 115°F. Remove the pineapple from the oven and cool to room temperature. Refrigerate for 12 hours before using.

SWEET-AND-SOUR REDUCTION
5 tablespoons Demerara sugar
1¼ cups red wine vinegar

Put sugar and vinegar in a heavy saucepan. Mix well and boil until it is reduced to the consistency of syrup, about 10 minutes. Remove from heat.

SESAME SALT
Equal parts white sesame seeds and coarse salt

Toast the sesame seeds in a frying pan over medium heat until golden and aromatic. Stir frequently to avoid burning. Cool and crush in a mortar with salt. Alternately, use a food processor, but be careful to pulse the seeds and salt gradually and not over-process to a paste.

POTATO LEAVES

4 to 6 large potatoes

Clarified butter, melted

Fine salt, to taste

Preheat oven to 275°F. Butter a baking sheet and line with parchment paper.

In a small bowl mix clarified butter and salt.

Using a mandoline, or your excellent knife skills along with a very sharp knife, slice the potatoes paper-thin. Arrange the slices on the baking sheet so that they overlap very slightly at the edges. Brush well with the butter mixture.

Bake until nicely golden and trim into uniformly sized rectangles approximately 1½ by 3 inches. Cool and store in an airtight container. If they are not crisp enough, you can put them back in the oven to dry out a little longer.

APRICOT-BEAN PURÉE

1 cup dried apricots

1 cup fresh small white beans

1 ham knuckle

1 onion, peeled

1 bouquet garni

Salt

Vinegar

Assorted small crunchy herbs and leaves
(basil, chives, mint, baby lettuce), washed and dried

In a small saucepan steam or boil the apricots until tender.

Bring a large saucepan of water to boil. Add the beans, the ham knuckle, onion, and bouquet garni and boil over medium heat until beans are tender.

Discard the ham knuckle and bouquet garni and purée beans and all their liquid while still warm in a blender with the apricots. Pass the purée through a fine strainer and season with salt and vinegar to balance the sweetness.

TO FINISH

Scoop out the foie gras in one piece if possible (or cut away the pineapple). Cut into approximately 1¼-by-2½-inch slices (or adjust to size slightly smaller than potato leaves). Sprinkle a little sesame salt on each slice of foie gras, then sandwich between 2 potato leaves. Repeat, creating a double-decker sandwich. Serve each sandwich on a plate decorated with lines of apricot purée and sweet-and-sour reduction, scattered with herbs and lettuce leaves.

• BEET RISOTTO WITH SAUTÉED BEET GREENS, LEEKS, BASIL OIL, PARMESAN, AND CHÊVRE •

The art of making a risotto depends upon patient, consistent additions of broth. If you start playing around with the heat, you can kiss your risotto good-bye. The trick is to find a medium-low flame where the rice absorbs the liquid at a steady rate, not too slow and not so fast that the liquid boils away before the rice has a chance to absorb it. You can never really predict how much broth you will use, so it's important NOT to follow exact amounts when making risotto. This makes a simple, elegant weekday dinner.

Serves 4 to 6

3 to 4 medium fresh red beets,
skin and stems intact, scrubbed
Olive oil

2-inch piece orange rind

1 clove garlic

1 large leek, rinsed well, dark green tops
sliced into ½-inch-thick pieces, plus one 1-inch piece
of the white bottom, chopped fine

6 to 8 cups chicken or vegetable broth,
preferably unsalted

3 large shallots, finely chopped

Salt and freshly ground black pepper

2 cups Italian Arborio rice
(American brands generally don't work)

¼ cup freshly grated Parmesan

4 ounces chêvre

Basil oil (recipe follows)

Preheat oven to 300°F.

Cut the beet greens off the beets, leaving about a 1-inch tail at the base intact. Wrap the beets in foil, taking care not to break the tails, as this will result in the loss of their sugary sweetness. Bake on the middle rack of the oven for 2 to 3 hours. No need to feel panicked—you won't kill the beets no matter how long you cook them; whether they're underdone or overdone, they will work for this recipe, but their texture will vary slightly. When done, the skin should appear dark, loose, and wrinkly and should peel easily away from the beet.

Remove the beets from the oven, cool and peel them, then cut into approximately ⅜-inch dice and reserve. If you're feeling really ambitious, you can cut the dice on a bias and produce ruby-like jewels, which make even more of a bang at the dinner table.

In a medium saucepan, bring 4 cups of water to a boil over high heat. Cut the thick stems off the beet leaves. Chop them into ¾-inch pieces and wash them well. Blanch the stems in boiling water until you can bite through them without getting stringy bits stuck between your teeth. Drain. Wash the leaves in several changes of water until the water comes clean. Blanch the leaves in boiling water for 1 to 2 minutes, or until the leaves wilt and the green color emerges. Drain.

Heat 2 tablespoons of olive oil in a skillet over high heat. Quickly add the orange rind and garlic and toss. Add beet stems and leaves and toss to coat with oil. Set aside in a bowl and cover to keep warm, discarding garlic and orange rind.

Cut the dark green part of the leek into ½-inch strips. Wipe out the skillet and heat 1 tablespoon of olive oil over very high heat. (If you cook the leeks over a low flame they will take on a slimy, unpleasant texture.) Throw in the leeks and sauté, stirring constantly, for 1 to 2 minutes, until the leeks are softened and just barely crispy at the edges. Remove from heat and set aside.

Heat the broth in a large pot and keep warm over a low flame, with a ladle handy.

Sauté the shallots and white leek bottom in olive oil on medium-high heat in a heavy-bottomed, 4- to 6-quart pot until translucent and slightly golden. Copper, if you have it, is dreamy for cooking risotto because it conducts heat well and evenly and the pot won't move when you stir it. Add a little salt and pepper to taste.

Add the rice and toss to coat well with the oil. Slowly start to add the broth, one ladleful at a time, stirring after each addition. Adjust the heat so the rice bubbles at a low but steady simmer.

Continue adding broth and stirring the rice until it is just soft to the bite, about 20 to 25 minutes. Add beets and beet greens and leeks once the rice is near to done. Remove from the heat and add Parmesan and chêvre; stir to mix. Serve with extra Parmesan and a generous drizzle of basil oil sprinkled on top.

BASIL OIL

1 bunch basil, leaves only

½ cup olive oil, chilled

Wash and dry basil. Heat 4 cups water to boil. Blanch basil in boiling water for 30 seconds. Immediately refresh in ice-cold water and drain when cool. Delicately squeeze dry.

Put the leaves in a blender. Add the olive oil and blend until mixed. Refrigerate for up to a day and strain. The color and flavor become more intense with time, but even an hour will give you a deliciously flavored oil. You should have a brilliant, emerald green oil.

• RED, PINK, AND ORANGE FRUITS WITH WHITE CHOCOLATE AND LEMON VERBENA •

This dessert is all about celebrating fruit—its many contrasting textures, aromas, juices, sweet and sour flavors. When composing a fruit plate such as this, you can't expect to fulfill a recipe's ingredient list, but must use your judgment in selecting the best, ripest fruits available. You won't be giving each guest a whole pomegranate or persimmon, so cut these larger fruits at the table right before you serve. Though generally I believe in sticking to seasonal fruits, occasionally it's exciting to prepare a wide and exotic assortment (which will most likely be available only at a specialty produce store). *Your choice of plate is important here, because you are really putting the fruit on exhibit. Avoid a plate that is too busy or colorful—a large jet black or bright white plate makes a lovely contrast. Provide each guest with their own smaller plate, and a sharp knife for peeling and cutting. A bowl for peelings can be offered individually or for the whole table.*

Serves 6

6 lychee nuts

18 to 24 cherries

1 pint currants

6 passion fruits

2 persimmons

1 small pomegranate

6 figs

12 ounces white chocolate, broken into individual pieces
(try to buy in chunk form)

1 sprig lemon verbena

Arrange fruits, white chocolate, and lemon verbena sprig on a plate and serve.

LYNETTE LATIOLAIS DAVIS

Public Relations Specialist

I have many childhood memories of foods, dishes, and tastes, but one of my most vivid memories is actually of a *process* rather than of a food. The process was making dirty rice, an especially savory Creole dish dense with flavor. Beyond being absolutely scrumptious and providing tasks little hands can do, it had the advantage of using things that might otherwise be thrown away, particularly chicken innards. That was a trait greatly appreciated by my Louisiana French family; indeed, Daddy used to say a French family could live on what an English family tossed out.

The enterprise was straightforward enough, a basic pilaf with flavorings; most world cuisines have an equivalent. We made a light stock from chicken (or turkey, or capon) giblets, including the heart and liver, along with sliced carrot, celery stick, onion (into which I got to stick two cloves), wing tips, and so on. When the stock had simmered long enough to be flavored water, we'd strain the solids and set aside the gizzards. Out came a heavy old iron meat grinder, the kind that attached to a counter. I would assemble the gizmo and vise it to a pullout chopping board.

Then began the real child labor: a grind of pungent onions, green peppers, and the cooked gizzards. The rice would be put into its cooking pot with a goodly amount of butter (always goodly amounts of butter in my family), stirred until the grains were well coated, then in went the flavored giblet water and the icky colored mush so earnestly ground by me. Stir, stir, stir, until all was well incorporated, big spoon of salt and vigorous grindings of black pepper, in which time the pot would come up to a boil, the burner turned way, way down, the rice pot's lid securely placed, and then wait for the delicious alchemy of dirty rice. Rice is satisfying and comforting, but this rice in particular, with its slightly spicy flavorings and hint of meat, as well as the knowledge that I was part of the making, all contributed to my interest in how to cook even at that young age.

Good cooking memories came from both sides of my family, and I was lucky enough to have a great-grandmother in my life until I was almost twelve years old. An original pioneer woman, she lived on a ranch in Rifle, Colorado, and, when widowed, continued to run it. For an urban child, the ranch was a strange and wondrous place. There were huge cider presses in the middle of a large apple orchard, a rickety building full of sawdust for keeping blocks of ice cut from the adjacent pond when frozen in wintertime, and another separate edifice whose sole purpose was to house the preserves Grandmother Mary put up. In that cool, slightly darkened room sat row upon row of sparkling jars filled with condiments of myriad colors and textures, from silky smooth apple butters to huge chunks of pickled watermelon rind, luscious apricot purées, light, clear amber apple jellies, preserved carrots, okra, and Blue Lake green beans. For some reason, Grandmother Mary always insisted on Blue Lake beans. Looking today through seed catalogues (surely one of the greatest cures for winter blues), I see it noted that of all the green beans featured, Blue Lake are the best for canning and preserving; obviously, my great-grandmother knew that from empirical experience.

There again, in the middle of a beautiful but remote land, children were involved in the production of food. We mounted ladders and picked ripe apricots, then split them apart barehanded. Sometimes we'd encircle forefinger and thumb around a particularly rosy apricot with the cleft in the middle so it looked like a bare bottom. Grandmother Mary would stew the apricots slowly for a very long time, then pour them into a tall conical strainer; with a wooden implement, we'd circle round and round within the strainer, apricot purée oozing through the tiny holes and draining into a large bowl, the fruit's pure essence glistening in a rich golden pond.

There was also high mountain fishing alongside any number of small lakes in the surrounding area, with vast quantities of trout caught and gutted by the men, then washed out and cooked by the women. I make the distinction between men's and women's chores because one of the funniest things my little brother (five or six years old at the time) ever said, after an especially successful fishing expedition was: "Tell the women we caught a lot of fish for them to cook." Some preferred their trout crusted in cornmeal, others dusted in flour, and a jar of bacon drippings always came along on these excursions to fry the trout in, all accomplished in a perfectly seasoned, blacker-than-black wonder of an old cast iron pan. Dredged in cornmeal or flour, I had no preference; the preparations were different from each other in chew, and I'd usually switch back and forth. An accompanying "lemon" squeeze was always from one of those plastic lemons, never a fresh lemon, which is to be expected in the middle of the wilds of Colorado; it was about the fishing, really.

I grew up with a family that didn't believe everything had to be on the table in no time flat. One of my father's favorite dishes was a drunken pork roast that took hours to cook, and boy was that worth the wait. Just as much as he loved making the dish—a pork butt browned in olive oil with half a gallon of Burgundy poured on top and left to simmer longly and slowly—he loved saying the dish in Italian: "Porco U-bri-A-co." My father was cooking because my parents divorced when I was not quite twelve years old, a positive move that would have been of even greater benefit to all involved had it been achieved a few years earlier. My father took on cooking in a good-natured way, though, and when shortcuts were necessary due to either time or financial constraints, a big bowl of buttered spaghetti was perfectly fine as long as there was fresh cheese to grate on top.

This was the era when the incomparable Julia Child began her *French Chef* program on PBS. Dad and I would watch it as often as dueling schedules allowed, cracking jokes and mimicking Julia's uproarious and utterly lovable affectations. Amusements aside, we were grateful students and really did try many dishes upon her inspiration. The first thing I ever made by myself was boeuf bourguignon, a long, involved dish that I followed step by step, meticulously, and was amazed at the result. Amazed, and hooked on cooking from that point on; it was probably one of the only times I've actually been impressed with myself.

The amazement came from being able to create something so utterly delicious and satisfying as much as from my pleasure in the process: the preparation and putting together of a red wine marinade with carrots and onions; parboiling the American bacon because who the heck knew what lardons were; creating a bouquet garni; sautéing mushrooms; parboiling and trimming the pearl onions (which, P.S., I don't do anymore, those frozen pearl onions are excellent); browning the floured beef bits; deglazing; recombining all and getting the simmer just perfect. A lovely subjective adventure, a safe and satisfying place to explore and experiment.

I was something of an anomaly in our upper-middle-class ghetto of Los Gatos, an hour south of San Francisco. My parents were divorced at a time when divorces were still somewhat rare, and then, I had chosen to live with my father instead of my mother, a bit of an eyebrow-raiser in our fairly conservative township. My siblings, who were four and five years younger than I, went to live with my mother, and they moved an hour north of San Francisco to Sonoma. My father desperately wanted to keep the children together and insisted I visit my mother and siblings for about a year after the divorce, but in my mind, they were always enemy camp.

Throughout high school, I continued to work my way through Julia Child's *French Chef* cookbook, and became proficient at cheese soufflés and all manner of quiches. My father was gone a great deal of the time because he had been made "redundant" at San Jose State College, where he had been a professor of English and American literature. He took on several jobs to keep the family solvent—he was paying child support and the dollars were always short. Working two, sometimes even three, part-time jobs kept him away a lot, and a comforting way to occupy myself after I'd completed my homework was to cook. Cooking became, in essence, something to fill emotional gaps, and provided a certain amount of solace at a troubling time.

Upon graduation from high school, I fled to San Francisco, desperate for cosmopolitanism. What a fabulous city for a young adult to test her new independence in, everything on a manageable scale—benignity, culture, and good food. My first apartment was on Nob Hill, a few blocks above Chinatown, which was an absolute boon for cash-strapped college students. You could eat well for five bucks, and do all your food shopping for the same amount. Why, if things were *really* bad, you could sit at a counter and have a bowl of rice and pot of tea for a buck. (Fortunately, things weren't ever that bad.)

As my college years unfolded, food and cooking continued to grow in importance. After my freshman year, an opportunity arose to attend a school in Sussex, England, the following year, and a summer spent Eurailing and hosteling seemed an excellent way to introduce myself to the European experience. I loved traveling alone, and made only a cursory travel plan in order to receive mail (and money, of course) at key American Express offices at the beginning of every month. I just wanted to wander and read, and read and wander. The possibility as well of immersing myself in a Continental food experience was entirely tantalizing.

I traveled up to a lovely, rustic hostel at Arcachon and Cap Ferrat, where I first learned how to make mayonnaise. The hostel was part of a campground, and I encountered a family in the communal kitchen that served both, making their meal of thinly sliced grilled steaks, *frites*, and "*une belle salade.*" They invited me to join them, and by the way, would you mind making the mayonnaise "*pour les frites?*" I had never known that mayonnaise was made from oil and egg yolks, and in this case a lot of elbow grease, as the camping ground/youth hostel "kitchen" was not equipped with an electric beater of any sort. But isn't that the best way to learn, the old-fashioned way? After some genial instruction, I produced a bowl of slightly loose mayonnaise to accompany our pan-fried *frites*; it was one of the most delicious things I'd ever eaten.

In fact, through the serendipity of a solo and unstructured travel plan, I ended up being "adopted" by a number of French people who brought me into their homes and shared their meals with me. Beyond the hand-whipped mayonnaise, I had my first experience with Camembert, and once I got past the odor—let's be honest, a well-ripened Camembert smells like an unwiped derrière—I loved the creamy, gamy unctuousness of its taste and texture. I watched in wonder as someone sopped their plate clean with baguette crusts after devouring fresh sliced tomatoes, chives, and olive oil. Everything, but simply everything, tasted better in France than it ever had in the States. Food there is less fooled with, comes faster and more directly from its source, and hasn't had every bit of taste bred out of it in the interest of prolonging shelf life. While it's true that *le supermarché* is becoming more prevalent in France, on recent trips I have found astoundingly beautiful, super-fresh, high-quality produce filling the aisles. The French wouldn't accept anything less, frankly. I will always love and be inspired by the profound affection the French have for well-prepared food, paired with appropriate wines.

It was easy to go to school in Europe, and inexpensive. I convinced my dad that a year at the Sorbonne would be just the ticket. I spent another summer traveling via Eurail Pass and staying in hostels, this time with a boyfriend from San Francisco who also had his sights set on living in Europe. We finished the summer in a *gîte* (a rustic home) on the northern coast of the Gironde outside Bordeaux, a little house smack in the middle of vineyards and cornfields that had no running water, a pump in the front yard, and an outhouse between rows of grapevines. Milk and eggs came from a farm next door, and all the rest of our groceries from a small town nearby to which we'd bicycle, usually on the days of the open-air *marché*. The townspeople found us very peculiar, but shared information nonetheless, the most important being to use the bundled vine cuttings stacked next to our house for grilling in the open fireplace. It became the only way we cooked for the month we were there, discovering a dozen different *buerres composés* to put on whatever our *grillade* was that evening. It was the best of living close to the land, eating things pulled out of the soil hours earlier, and drinking superb *vins du terroir*.

In the fall, we were lucky to find a spartan little studio in Paris's Fifth Arrondissement; it had a small, two-burner stove incorporating a tiny temperamental oven, and a shower in the kitchen, which meant we brushed our teeth in the same sink we washed and prepared vegetables in. The toilet—euphemistically referred to as a Turkish loo, with two elevated footprints and a hole—was out on the landing, and we shared it with the adjacent apartment. There was no fridge, but there was a large square at our Métro stop where a good open-air market took place three times a week, so we bought food every other day.

It was an intoxicating time. I loved my program at the Sorbonne, and as a student could eat very inexpensively in a multitude of restaurants. I continued to teach myself to cook, an easy and pleasurable enterprise in Paris, where food and dining are perpetually front and center. The boyfriend who'd come to be with me in France decided to follow a course of study in the culinary arts. He lined up an *apprentissage en cuisine* that would begin late spring, but first he needed to learn the language. One of his methods for augmenting his language studies was to read and cook his way through *Larousse Gastronomique*, so beyond increasing my repertoire of skills and dishes that year in Paris, I began to understand and assimilate cooking theory as well. Whenever possible, I'd attach myself to whichever of my French friends was cooking, just to observe, in exchange offering services as a kitchen slave and *garde manger*, i.e., a vegetable peeler. Ultimately, cooking is not unlike a language: you need to arrive at a point where you *think* in that language rather than translate in your mind before you speak.

In Paris, it's virtually impossible to find a French person unwilling to talk about food and recipes. The food shops and open-air markets are libraries full of information, every shop owner and purveyor, not to mention the lady standing in front or back of you in line, is ready with a suggestion or recipe. A favorite chicken fricassee comes from a butcher in Paris, and I got a hands-on lesson in cleaning and de-bearding mussels from a craven old man who thought, as did most Parisians I met, that because I appreciated their culture I was worth investing time in. The understanding the French have of good food and wine was something that helped ground me, helped clarify ideas about what I sought in life, who I wanted to be. It merely underlines my sybaritism that I feel so much of what is really important in life goes on around the kitchen and at a dining table, but I really do.

Those formative years of adopting cooking as a definer of self, truly studying French, and later Italian, cuisine, have continued to be a mainstay of self in adulthood, married life, and parenthood. Cooking is always and ever a comforting, satisfying activity. As widely reported, after September 11 many and sundry good cooks and dabblers alike took to kitchens to make long, slow, involved dishes, things taking two or three days to cook, like cassoulets. I made a huge pot of stock, as well as a new batch of Bolognese sauce. But the fact remains that people, women, mothers, cook less and less, so time-constrained are modern lives. But cook I must; it's important to keep the proverbial home fires burning, and I cook several times a week for family meals, in addition to a meal with friends over the weekend.

To my great pleasure, my preadolescent son is now showing an interest in cooking, and often makes himself available for herb chopping and vegetable peeling. He's learning how to use a knife, and is an excellent polenta stirrer. Additionally, he likes, God bless, sauce. My husband does not like sauce (serves himself my near-perfect *blanquettes de veau* with a slotted spoon), but the son *does* like sauce, which I have many variations on in my freezer: deep red wine and morel sauces from beef roasts; a lighter sauce with chanterelles from a recent veal roast, as well as leftover bits of sauce from osso buco; a short tub of stock to deglaze a pan. The son likes a snack of *pastina in brodo* that he can make himself, simply by putting a large, frozen tub of stock in a pan with *stelline* or orzo over medium heat; the pasta is cooked by the time the stock has unfrozen and come to a boil. He also enjoys pulling the always-present chunk of *Parmigiano-Reggiano* out of the fridge, pulling off a few large morsels to eat with or without crackers. It is always worthwhile trying everything out on your kids; they come around to most things at some point or another. We present our son with many things that are beyond his full comprehension, but I believe there's a large storage area in brains for all these impressions and experiences. As children grow and become more engaged with the outside world, these sensory experiences will be called out of storage and find usefulness and resonance in their lives.

I'm proud to have the cooking know-how to pull together a good and tasty meal. Sadly, too many people are afraid to roll up their sleeves and cook. We don't have the fine sensibilities of the French and Italians where people who have never "learned" to cook can still defend themselves in the kitchen because the basics are simply ingrained in their DNA. Cooking should be a life discipline. You can set out to learn just four or five dishes and consider these your discipline. It's neither complicated nor daunting, and it is so very, very satisfying.

I will always cook; it's a way to honor someone. Time spent in the kitchen, sharing whatever has come your way that day while peeling carrots or shelling peas, washing lettuce and making a little dressing, is a valuable way to apportion time together. Arriving at the dinner table, there's more to discuss and food to share. It's ultimately what most of us hope for in life: pleasurable time together.

· BOEUF BOURGUIGNON ·

Julia quite rightly states: "When beef stew is in the oven, all's right with the world, and beef Bourguignon is the best beef stew known to man." She goes on to note, as do others, that in fact the dish improves with a day's "marriage," and that it's a great dish to make for dinner parties because you can have everything pretty much done before guests arrive, and spend time chatting instead. Accompaniments can be as simple as quickly steamed green beans or peas, buttered noodles, and a green salad that the French would happily just toss on the same dinner plate after the bourguignon had been sopped up with a nice crust of bread.

An approximate recipe

Salt pork

Olive oil

Stewing beef

Salt and pepper

Red wine

Beef stock

Bay leaf

Bouquet garni or fresh thyme sprigs

Tomato paste or plum tomatoes

Garlic

Mushrooms

Butter

Pearl onions

Sugar, if desired

Beurre manié (recipe within)

Parsley

Ingredients vary rarely, but count on a ½ pound of stewing beef per person (perhaps an extra half pound for the leftover amount you'll freeze and keep for some wintry day . . .). Do make the effort to get salt pork instead of using American bacon and a reasonable bottle of substantive red wine. For the garnish, a pound of fresh mushrooms (I actually prefer cremini as opposed to champignons de Paris) and pearl onions; don't even think of parboiling and peeling your own unless you have oodles of time on your hands; the frozen ones (not creamed, obviously) work perfectly.

Cut your big piece of salt pork into bite-size chunks and brown in a small bit of olive oil in the casserole in which you'll be doing the entire boeuf bourguignon. The lardons will produce more fat, which will be for browning the beef bits. (If you're using American bacon, make sure it's thick-sliced and parboil to remove most of the smokiness. You could use pancetta instead.)

Remove lardons with a slotted spoon, set aside in a bowl, and begin browning the beef chunks, which you've salted and peppered. There are differing schools on whether one should flour the beef bits, and I often do, as recommended by *Larousse Gastronomique*. Others, Richard Olney for instance, have you throw a handful of flour on top of the beef after all the bits are browned. I don't find it makes a difference one way or t'other, because I always use a *buerre manié* at the end anyway to get the dish to the thickness I want.

When all bits of beef pieces are browned (do this in batches, never crowd, otherwise they steam and fail to attain a nice crust), pour the browning oil out, add the red wine to the casserole, at least three-quarters of the bottle, have a sip yourself, and with a good wooden spoon scrape the bottom of the casserole to get all the nice bits of meat caramelization incorporated into the liquid. Put all beef and salt pork pieces back into casserole, and top up with beef stock to make certain all the meat pieces are covered.

Add the bay leaf, *bouquet garni* or several sprigs of thyme, a spoon of tomato paste or two small or plum tomatoes (this will completely incorporate into the stew), and a few peeled and lightly smashed garlic cloves. Bring to a low simmer and cook either stovetop or in the oven for at least 2 hours, to upwards of 3.

For the garnish, clean the mushrooms, trim the stems and cut in quarters. Sauté at high heat in a combination of butter and olive oil; it's nice to try and achieve a bit of crustiness on the mushroom quarters. Set aside.

In another sauté pan, put in 1 or 2 tablespoons of butter, and at least 1 to 1½ cups of small pearl onions. A smidgen of sugar can be added if desired. Cook on a medium-low heat, shaking occasionally, to brown the onions a bit. Make a *buerre manié* (mix equal parts flour and butter together, then form into balls) at this time as well. Wash well and chop a large handful of parsley (if serving the boeuf bourguignon presently).

When the beef has simmered for 2 to 3 hours, test to make certain the beef pieces are quite tender, and skim whatever fat has risen to the surface. Pull out the garlic cloves unless they've disintegrated, as well as the bouquet garni or bay leaf and thyme branches. Ladle off about 1 cup of the sauce into the *buerre manié*, then put the entirety back into the boeuf bourguignon casserole. Stir to commingle all well.

Add the onions and mushrooms, stir all, scraping down sides of casserole, and put to simmer again over medium-low heat for a short time. You are then ready to serve, or else let cool, and reheat later. If leaving overnight, of course refrigerate.

My personal preference is nice buttered noodles as an accompaniment, along with whatever vegetable you like. A very pretty plate is the boeuf bourguignon sprinkled with bright green chopped parsley, and baby carrots alongside. Other serving suggestions are boiled and buttered potatoes or mashed potatoes, toast points, or rice. And yes, bottles of good red wine to wash it all down with.

• THE DAY AFTER THANKSGIVING GUMBO •

This is a marvelous treatment for all the leftover turkey, and gumbo is so flexible that you can pretty much play with this as your taste desires.

Another approximate recipe

Leftover turkey

2 to 3 onions

3 to 4 sticks celery

2 to 3 carrots

2 to 3 green peppers

10 or more cloves garlic

3 to 4 jalapeño peppers

2 to 3 medium tomatoes, peeled, seeded, and diced

1 cup oil or bacon drippings

1 cup all-purpose flour

Okra (optional)

Bay leaf

Thyme

Oregano

Ground black and white and cayenne pepper

Andouille sausage (optional)

Cooked rice for serving

Parsley or green onions, chopped

Gumbo filé powder (optional)

Dismantle the turkey, cutting as much meat off the bone as possible (hope the oysters are still there); place all deboned meat in a large bowl and refrigerate until needed.

Take the turkey carcass and all bones left from the dismantling and throw in a large stockpot with a quartered onion and some slices of celery and carrots, to make a broth. Cook for about 1 hour, until the turkey stock has developed enough brothy flavor. Strain and set aside.

While the broth is cooking, do all prep work for the gumbo base: prepare 1 to 2 large onions, several celery sticks, green peppers, garlic, and jalapeño (or others of equal heat) peppers, all chopped in medium dice, all seeds removed and discarded, and tomatoes.

Make the roux, which is the irreplaceable core and basis of gumbo, in a very large, heavy-bottomed casserole or stockpot. And have patience, stir slowly and longly. I personally like mine to arrive at an almost walnut color, but make certain not to let the roux burn. I've cooked a roux for as long as a half hour, and if you're standing close by the stove, doing all the vegetable prep work simultaneously, it works out fairly well. Standard measurements would be 1 cup oil to 1 cup flour. As to the oil used, I've actually used olive oil before (don't tell the Southern aunties) and it tasted delicious, but bacon drippings, of which I always keep a container in the freezer, are traditional.

If you're using okra, here's a great way to remove the sliminess: wash and cut okra in finger-width slices, and dry sauté in a nonstick pan. Set aside along with all other prepped vegetables, and keep stirring that roux!

When the roux has arrived at a color you like, first add the chopped onion and stir for a while, then the celery, then all the peppers. Now add your turkey stock, the tomatoes, okra, and a few small spoonfuls of dried herbs, including bay leaves, thyme, oregano, and a combination of ground peppers— black, white, and a smidgen of cayenne if desired. Other heat in the gumbo will come from the jalapeño peppers, and I always add one or two smoked andouille sausages in thick slices that have been quartered at this point, as well.

Simmer for 45 minutes to 1 hour, add the turkey meat, and cook another 30 minutes at least or until thick and flavorful. Similar to *boeuf bourguignon*, gumbo can sit and marry for a day, and be even better.

Always, gumbo is served in deep bowls with a mound of rice in the middle; make certain your table setting includes a big soup spoon. A pretty sprinkle of either chopped parsley or green onion tops is a nice color complement. Gumbo filé powder is passed separately and sprinkled on top as an added thickening agent, although purists will say it's *either* okra or filé powder, never the two together. Well, I do what I want, so for me it's usually both.

As noted above, gumbo offers a marvelously creative palette, so if you like seafood in your gumbo, by all means add shrimp or oysters during the last few minutes of cooking time. It's about whatever you've got a hankering for. I've also found the best way to make a gumbo is to open up three or four books to their gumbo recipes, and work from them all. Jeremiah Tower's *New American Classics*, which was written while he was the chef and owner of Stars restaurant in San Francisco, has a marvelous recipe that uses smoked duck as well as prawns. Obviously, Paul Prudhomme's *Louisiana Kitchen* has great gumbo recipes, as do the *Commander's Palace*, *River Road*, and *Times-Picayune Creole* cookbooks. Another beautiful and atmospheric little book is from a marvelous old plantation outside of Lafayette, Louisiana, called *The Shadows-on-the-Teche* cookbook, but you'd likely have to visit in order to find the book. But all in all, with gumbo, license and creativity, after the basics, are what's fun, and tasty.

MICHELLE LATIOLAIS

Professor of English, University of California at Irvine

I have always been surrounded by good cooks, and by people who paid attention to what their loved ones were eating. I remember my mother once saying to my brother, "I didn't make those bones so that you could ruin them playing football." In fact, I don't remember my brother ever playing anything but tennis—and like a gazelle, as he is very tall, six-four, and thin, and tends to leap about rather balletically— but obviously the idea of a sport more brutal had been floated, if not engaged in. My mother's comment was not one of those I-spent-forty-eight-hours-in-labor-with-you comments; it was merely a simple statement of the value of his body in its present good state, and a reminder not to be stupid about its care and preservation. Much of her aesthetic of food followed along these lines: one prepared and ate real food, lots of legumes and grains and fresh vegetables and fruits, food that was nourishing and pleasing to one's body. There were no armies of vitamin bottles or "health bars," which she would have scoffed at, and there were few boxes or packages in our cupboards.

"Food is not square," my mother would say. We drank gallons of whole milk, slathered pounds of butter on French bread, and ate on many a summer evening cobs of fresh sweet white corn—silver, really, which my mother favored—and platters of beefsteak tomatoes sliced as thick as, well, beefsteak. She dressed the tomatoes with good olive oil and ground fresh pepper over them and often would not even salt them. My brother and I would liberally salt them once they were put before us and she would occasionally stay a hand, saying, "Careful, baby, don't kill their freshness." The corn and tomatoes came from a farmer in Sonoma near the high school and he often grew Blue Lake green beans, too, which my mother always tossed with bacon fat and bits of bacon. We were all as thin as rails.

Other mothers would often ask my mother how she got us to eat vegetables as happily as we did, and she unabashedly claimed that there were few vegetables a child wouldn't eat if you put butter and freshly ground pepper over them. She believed in freshly ground pepper, and she believed in nurturing good eating habits, and she believed in the pleasure and beauty of what she termed "honest" food. She did not believe in picky eaters, nor would she ever cater much to one if he or she had the bad manners to voice aversion, and consequently we happily stood in the kitchen and asked what she was making and how long it would take and what we could do.

The idea of work in the kitchen was not anything that invoked resistance in my brother or me. We grated cheese and sliced small Japanese cucumbers and peeled potatoes and sorted beans and understood that meat was washed well and then dried. We knew how to be helpful in the kitchen, and we liked not being infantilized, and we talked about homework and politics, always politics. This was Northern California and Vietnam was going on and my brother's bones were in contention on this other front as well. Christopher was not going to *that* war, the only issue I remember my parents in agreement on. They had been divorced since I was six, my brother five. (We have an older sister, Lynette, who lived with our father, but we saw her only two or three times over the next ten years.) My father had made all the arrangements for my brother to attend the University of Guadalajara if the war was still going on when Chris had to register for the Selective Service.

I remember these political conversations over dinners of homemade chili with

big chunks of shredded beef, or wine roast and long-grain white rice that was mois-
tened with unthickened wine sauce, a sauce as thin and runny as wine itself. We
loved it, particularly the rice, as we added butter to this with the sauce. I remember
my mother cooking the roast in a pressure cooker, and though she must have cooked
it when she got home from work, I feel a memory of it cooking all day, too, and the
kitchen smelling yeasty, the way it does when wine is being cooked down. The roast
was a mean cut of meat, bottom round or chuck, and shaped like a squared-off football, and as far from showing signs of "marbling" as Formica. It had to be cooked,
and cooked a long time, but several cups of Gallo Burgundy did their level best to
tenderize its sinews and worked its magic even more explicitly on our desire to have
sophisticated palates, to drink wine. We were growing up in wine country, after all,
and though we couldn't legally drink, our mother always let us have sips, even a
small glass of beer here or there for my brother. Wine roast for dinner was like getting to drink wine, and my mother would never understand how you could take her
son's body at eighteen for war, but you wouldn't allow him a drink until he was
twenty-one. I now realize wine roast was a dish of civil disobedience, one which allowed my mother to give us our leash but which also allowed us to wake up the next
morning without any sign of having imbibed a drop.

Wine roast was a winter dish, and my mother was always quite conscious of the
seasons and what was in season and what was good and light when it was hot outside and what was comforting and substantial when it was cold. After my mother
married my stepfather, Milo, in the winter we had King Bolete mushrooms and
chanterelles and even a rarer coral mushroom, all of which Milo hunted on his
ranch and brought into the house in a basket, dirt filtering down through its reeds
onto the floor as he entered and no one caring, as *Look at the size of that Boletus* was
all anyone was thinking. As I understand it, the King Bolete is a type of porcini and
if that is true, then the California version is milder, subtler in its flavor than the
porcini I have eaten in Italy. Some years there were lots of chanterelles, and morning after morning while they lasted I went off to school with a chanterelle omelet in
my stomach.

I had no idea a chanterelle mushroom was anything fancy until I left home and started to work in San Francisco in the restaurant business to put myself through college. That people paid huge sums of money to eat chanterelles amazed me, and yet I had never taken them for granted. Some years Milo would come in from hunting and shake his head. "Just aren't many this year," he'd say sadly. "Conditions have to be perfect," and like so much having to do with the way I grew up with food, it wasn't about money. It was about time and rain and sunlight and who had put in the effort to peel the wild asparagus or pound that abalone some friend of my stepfather's had just fished from up near Marshall and left on the porch. Food entailed work, effort, attention, and I remember this work and effort and attention as one of the most enthralling and joyful aspects of my childhood.

"No child of mine" was an expression I grew up hearing a lot, and certainly no child of my mother's went off to school without breakfast. A child sitting in school even mildly hungry conjured up for her brain malfunction, or at the very least inattention; if you were hungry you would not think of algebra or the electoral college— you would think about food. My mother always worked full-time, and yet she made pancakes on weekday mornings, and these often covered in gravy. She made sherried eggs over toast, and even creamed tuna over toast. She was resourceful, keeping batter in the fridge and gravy from the night before, which she loosened with milk as she warmed it up. If we'd had beans and rice for dinner, we had huevos rancheros a few mornings hence; if there was French bread left over, she'd make milk toast with poached eggs and a pool of melting butter all floating in warm milk. We loved this breakfast, and I can still see the black specks of ground pepper against the white milk, which is why I've known the expression *une mouche en lait* since before I can remember. "Beauty mark," my mother always noted, putting the milk toast down before us; *a fly in milk,* that was how the French said it, and we thought that enormously amusing and laughed and I think somehow associated our breakfast with the marvelous affectation of beauty marks and powdered wigs and grand châteaux.

These gifts of my childhood were only in part about place, the wine country of Northern California, the bounty this land presented, because I think in greater measure was the gift of know-how, of willing effort, call it technique, even expertise. I do not remember anyone ever saying to me, "Oh, that's adult food," or "You won't like that," or "That takes too long to make," or any implication that I was too young to eat something and then to learn to like it or appreciate it, or too young and uncoordinated to be able to prepare some kind of food. Did I struggle in learning how to make deviled eggs, how to nudge the hard-boiled yolk from the white without tearing the white? You bet, and did I make many a pie crust that would have better served as roofing? You bet. But I made those crusts at age six and seven and by the age of eleven had learned not to overhandle the dough and was making a pretty good crust, and in about twenty minutes' time. No one said, "That's a good crust *for a kid*," as the only standard ever operable was my great-grandmother's pie crusts. There were no degrees of accomplishment in the kitchen, no condescension to a junior cook.

When I was fourteen, Christopher got me a job at the Au Relais restaurant in Sonoma, and this allowed me some financial mobility, allowed me to work around beauty and food and the very charged theater of dining in a fine and popular restaurant. The Au Relais was a modest turn-of-the-century house that had been converted into a lovely restaurant. On Friday, Saturday, and Sunday evenings throughout my two and a half years of high school, I was a busgirl there, and Saturday and Sunday mornings I cleaned the restaurant and worked in the kitchen doing prep. One sign of accomplishment in the Au Relais kitchen was the ability to beat three or four quarts of heavy cream into whipped cream with a balloon whisk. I learned at the Au Relais to make a cream that would billow on the plate, falling sensuously from the spoon, not stand at attention as though paralyzed—cream à la Frank Gehry rather than Donald Trump.

When I was seventeen, I declared financial independence on my tax return, which you could do in those pre-Reagan days. I registered at San Francisco State University, found an apartment for a hundred dollars a month and first one restaurant job and then another and then another so that I had three jobs and was attending classes full time. On my own, away from long-divorced but ever-dueling parents, I sought out my sister, Lynette, whose address on Taylor Street I'd had for some time but had never made use of. One Saturday morning, I showed up on her doorstep, unannounced and most decidedly unwelcome. And yet, because it was Saturday, shopping-in-Chinatown day, Lynette put her dismay aside, and we made our way down the hill onto sidewalks amassed with people pushing through blocks whose curbs were lined with cages of live ducks and chickens and turtles, and whose shops displayed pallets of fish on ice, and expanses of vegetables and squashes and melons, most of which I did not know the names of. San Francisco's Chinatown was my first exposure to an open-air farmers market, and because of this, I always associate them with Lynette.

Nowadays, on Tuesdays, I go to the farmers market in Culver City, a part of Los Angeles well south of Hollywood and Beverly Hills, an area once grasslands and the site of some of California's first movie studios. I am particularly fond of this market, which I call the writers' farmers market because it starts at three in the afternoon, after I have spent the morning and early afternoon working. I am usually driven there by Hartford, a graduate student who has become a friend, a man with Southern roots and so a man who knows how to "visit," to spend time with someone not his own age and to enjoy it . . . or at least to act convincingly as though he does. He has kind blue eyes, a deep, mirthful laugh, and an easiness with the world that offsets my irritableness. During the years I have known Hartford, he's lost his father to cancer and his grandmother to the ravages of time; he adores his mother and his younger sister, Teddy; and these losses and affections give him a seriousness and a receptivity that are at work on our trips to the market and our exchanges there.

Hartford picks me up in his Subaru station wagon at three P.M. and we're off, wending our way through various neighborhoods, avoiding Los Angeles traffic, and we arrive at the market just a few minutes later. Certainly, there is discussion in the car as to what we prepared with last weeks' purchases—"Those blackberries were awesome," says Hartford, looking across the car. Berries are often two or three for some amount, three boxes of strawberries for seven dollars, say, and blackberries two boxes for four dollars. Because Hartford is buying for one, oftentimes I'll buy three boxes, give Hartford one, or vice versa, he'll buy blackberries and give me one box.

I have a job in academia, which means I have the luxury of being able to allot my time how I please, and so much of the difficulty that working people have today with buying and preparing good food, I do not have. I help run a very small writing program in southern California, and I am able to attend farmers markets, particularly ones that start at three in the afternoon on Tuesdays, and I am able to be at home and to have something cooking on the stove while I work, or to bake, or to just generally have time for the process that cooking entails, a process within whose interstices I can accomplish that for which I am paid. Also, I do not have children, which means that I do not spend weekday afternoons driving from schoolyards to lessons and soccer fields and malls. My life allows for something that I think a lot of lifestyles don't today, and for this I am extremely grateful, and lucky. I think I am supposed to feel sidelined by not having children, by not being part of the importance of this mad dash here with the kids, that mad dash there, but I don't. Every woman I know complains good-heartedly about the chauffeur service she provides her children. The woman across the street who is a painter complains—good-heartedly—that she has lost the entire summer ferrying her children about from golf courses to soccer fields. I suppose many women prefer being lashed to the steering wheel instead of the kitchen butcher block, but it seems to me a puzzling commentary on feminism and contemporary life. So many issues here. But finally what I am saying is that I have time to cook, that I am sprung free of the gridding that American life now asks of our days.

It's late summer or early fall at the market, and though there are still plums and even peaches, and those newfangled orbs called pluots, they are not good, and Hartford and I do not buy them. We favor a French vendor who grows varieties of small melons and heirloom tomatoes and calls out, "All organic here, folks, all organic," in his French accent. He wears purple corduroy cutoffs over longer stretch pants, and a straw cowboy hat beaded and feathered, and with that unerring aesthetic of the French, he's as fashionable and colorful as a page in the Sundance catalog. He sells ambrosias and *charentais* and rocky sweets and he will pick out melons to "eat tomorrow, eat Thursday, eat Friday" if you ask him to. I have served these melons with cookies for dessert, and my guests have sat there amazed, having not tasted for years a melon sun-ripened, perfumey with flavor. Though Hartford and I usually hit the French melon vendor last because melons are heavy, today we select our melons immediately and ask him to hold them. The weather has been so erratic this summer that some Tuesdays he's had melons, and some Tuesdays he's had only tomatoes, and even those are sparser, less bountiful than late summer usually offers. "Thirty years organic, folks," he calls as we leave. "Thirty years organic."

One of the joys of frequenting farmers markets rather than a supermarket is the schooling one receives in the seasons, a return to the excitement attendant upon a certain time of year: strawberry time, or that time in the summer when the peaches are in, the apricots and plums, and later still, after it's been hot enough, the succulent tomatoes and melons, and finally the apples are back, and Brussels sprouts appear and fall starts to deepen and there are pumpkins and gourds and acorn squash, celeriac. What is learned from things having their time, what is prepared for and anticipated and then embraced because of time, is not a lesson that should be lost. We live in a time when we need not emotionally progress past the impulse control of two-year-olds; anything can be had at any time of year, and yet, not only do we lose a calendar that reflects life and death, our own cycles, the rightness of those cycles, we lose even more drastically authenticity, what an un-gassed tomato really tastes like, or how a strawberry ripened by the sun explodes with juice in your mouth versus one that has decomposed to something vaguely flavored and pliant and red.

And as a teacher, I would say that what is lost in eliding the seasons is patience. I think we have a very unreal sense of the efficacy of computers in creating and nurturing skills in students, and we certainly think computers are microwave ovens, speeding up the process of learning. But an apprenticeship in writing takes time, has its seasons; the fruit that emerges must be tended for it to grow and ripen . . . and sometimes it doesn't ripen for a very long time. You have to write so much failed work, so much juvenilia before the better writing emerges, before there's a spring and a ripening into summer and palatability.

Hartford and I scoot down the market to the hydroponic lettuce grower whose lettuces are as beautiful as flowers, were flowers deep green and red-tinged. In fact, there does happen to be a green rose with reddish-pink tinges, but the lettuces are prettier, blowsier. I have been known to walk out into the living room when guests are there to show them one of these small heads of lettuce before pulling the leaves apart. They are baby lettuces—or lettuces cut early, or rather just at the right time: oak leaf, Batavia, romaine, green and red leaf, Bibb, and I usually buy all the varieties but truly love the more toothsome Batavia, which is nutty and substantial and as deserving of prized extra-virgin olive oils as any leaf can be. I buy enough at the farmers market for the week for my husband, Paul, and myself, and perhaps a dinner party or two. Were it not for Paul's love of vinegars, and guests, I'd probably eat the baby Batavia with only good olive oil and salt and freshly ground pepper, but then again, I am blessed with a husband who will eat main-course salads for dinner. He is also grandly tolerant when I march into the living room to show someone just how beautiful a *head of lettuce* can be. These lettuces are sold with their roots completely intact and will last—if they must—for up to two weeks in the refrigerator if left this way. Sometimes a person will have never seen a lettuce with its long thin roots like a wizard's beard. "Oh wise and magical lettuce," I say, laughing. Merlin with a hat to rival the Queen Mum's.

Once Hartford and I have staked our claim to the produce we know we want, we start to look around, to shop the market more systematically. We pass the lavender man in his denim bib overalls and dreadlocks. He, too, has his patter: "Lavender, yeah lavender, smell me, come on and tell me, talk to me, walk with me, lavender, talk with me, lavender." Hubert Selby Jr. said in an interview once that New York City had a music all its own, which was always there and audible and pulsing, and that Los Angeles had no music. I think this is true until you walk the farmers market, and there is the jazz quartet playing and the patter of the vendors and the children running from sample bin to sample bin, chomping on bits of Pink Lady apples and slices of mandarins and satsumas, even plastic spoonfuls of pomegranate seeds, which amuse them no end. I watch a child, her long blond ringlets falling forward, stick a toothpick very, very carefully into a piece of persimmon and raise it to her lips as though it might be poison, as though it might be chocolate. She chews, and for a time she is not sure, but then she nods her head with an interior affect—no one is there with her—and finishes her first taste of persimmon, swallows, and goes on to the Fuji apple samples. "Okay, I tried," you can see her saying to some adult in her mind who has said "Try everything once."

The winter squashes are coming in and there are huge, vividly orange chunks of kabocha and a squash called *calabaza de Castilla*. If you know the science, it's as though that color is the vegetal world's neon for *beta-carotene, beta-carotene, beta-carotene*. I buy a chunk of the *calabaza de Castilla* for two dollars to make a soup or purée, something to have in the freezer to go with pork chops or a quick steak. It is a chunk half the size of Castile, Spain, and Hartford and I start to regret that I didn't bring my cart.

One of our favorite organic growers has three colors of Swiss chard, and Hartford and I talk about a very simple soup Paul makes out of *Marcella's Italian Kitchen*, a soup whose stock is the water the chard is steamed in, flavored with garlic, rosemary, and a few anchovies. It's a delicious soup, and when Hartford demurs, I tell him he won't be able to taste the anchovies, nor should he tell people they're in there until they've finished their bowls. An appreciation for certain foods, like much fine writing, needs to be taught, or we need someone to expose us to it, to ease our way, to nudge us gently off our usual feed. A few weeks later, when I give Hartford a bowl of this soup, which Paul and I have made the night before, he finishes the bowl with gusto. His willingness makes me very happy, and he borrows the cookbook.

Writing is a process, and one whose work must be embraced with *some* joy, because if not, it's too painful, and cooking also, of course, is a process and one that asks for the joyful embrace of work. I find these two processes mesh beautifully, *embrace* each other, to overuse a word. Writing is cerebral and incurs an exhaustion that is offset, evaporated even, with rising to stir a pot of moccasin beans or to put a soup through the food mill or to now roll out those cookies whose dough has been resting in the refrigerator. Writing, like many a stew or a chili, is enhanced with time. Not only are writing and cooking things that enfold and evolve over time, time itself—hang time, tempering time—is something it must be allowed. My sablée cookie dough, a recipe from my friend Andy Tsuji, in order for the flour to absorb the butter, needs to rest, and writing, in order for you to hear the cadences clearly, to see certain infelicities, needs time to rest also. Taste a Oaxacan mole just after you've finished it and the flavors will seem discordant, weird; taste it tomorrow and your brow raises in delight. That you've spent hours gathering upward of forty different ingredients seems merely the work of a moment . . . that you've spent twenty years learning the language so that you could write that one paragraph, ah, poof, a nanosecond. In eating, as in reading, there are hundreds of years, thousands, brought to bear on one moment, and in that moment of consumption, in that moment of perception, we are projected into infinitude. Joy has no clock, and so the paltry and not-so-paltry amounts of time we expend in struggling to make these moments is an offering I am willing to make.

The man at the farmers market we buy Swiss chard from had earlier in the summer sold lemon cucumbers, and he had been amazed I knew what they were. He's an older man with a craggy Western face, and I tell him that I grew up in the wine country in Northern California and that my stepfather always grew lemon cucumbers in his garden. I tease the man about his lemon cucumbers being a little big, tell him my stepfather insisted on picking them about the size of a lime. He tells me next week he'll bring them smaller for me, and the next week he does, and I tell a few people standing around how we always prepared them in Sonoma, and it's odd when not one of them reaches in the box to grab a few to take home. The vegetable man throws up his hands and laughs, and so do I. Later, Paul says maybe people don't have knives that cut thinly; maybe people don't like raw white onion; maybe people don't use olive oil or have a pepper grinder. Maybe. I know that if someone stood there and told me how to prepare something, I wouldn't be able to leave without buying the item whose preparation they'd just instructed me in. I'm used to the writers in my program upon whom nothing is lost: note takers, collectors of words and processes and experiences, avatars of curiosity, dusty with the work of the desk.

Our weather has been strange, and Paul has said that soup sounds good to him. I buy four small heads of cauliflower for a buttermilk-and-cauliflower soup flavored with dill out of *Food and Wine's Soups and Stews* cookbook. The dill comes from a Chinese family whose bundles of Thai basil and flat-leaf parsley and cilantro and lemongrass are as big as sprays of gladioli. Each bunch is one dollar and has been picked only an hour or two earlier. From the Chinese family I also buy a few chilies—pasillas, serranos, jalapeños—for a pot of beans with tequila, *frijoles borrachos,* "drunken beans," as Rick Bayless calls them, though perhaps they have been called this by Mexicans for centuries. I buy Pink Lady and Sundowner apples; I buy walnuts and a bag of tangerines, all organic. I am happy with all the beautiful shades of orange at the market today, the persimmons, the squash, the citrus, and the reds of the pomegranates and the varieties of apples. I look at the stall where dates are sold—Medjools, Zahidi, Halawy, Deglet Noor—and I think of the barbecue sauce for pork tenderloin given to me by Hartford, a family recipe made with shallots and dates and maple syrup.

I am generally lucky in my graduate students, and I enjoy them immensely, and especially working with them and their work, but there are particular students who become friends, and who allow me to be a representation of something very old and for the most part lost. If Hartford has ever been bored listening to me tell him how to fix lemon cucumbers or how to make soup with Swiss chard, I've not been able to detect it, but somehow *boredom* is what older people have become for younger people today, and it just seems understood that older people and being around them will be boring, useless, a waste of time. That Hartford not only takes the time to come fetch me every Tuesday but also to take down recipes and give me some in return is a touchstone in my week, and in a much broader sense, too. There is something vital that older people pass on to younger and that is how to care for one another's bodies, how to soothe them and nurture them and keep them, while we can, from dying. This seems to be something in the American culture that we are losing. No amount of bought food, no matter its quality, will ever replace the food—often very simple—that someone has prepared for us and placed before us.

· PERSIMMON COOKIES ·

For this recipe, use the large, acorn-shaped persimmons called hachiyas. *Use very plump, ripe ones, very soft. Don't go to the bother of putting the pulp in a blender, just make sure there are no big chunks. Use a fork to mash if needed, but the persimmons should be so ripe that this is basically unnecessary.*

Makes approximately 4 dozen cookies

1 cup *hachiya* persimmon pulp

1 teaspoon baking soda

1 cup softened butter

1 cup sugar

1 egg

1 teaspoon vanilla

2 cups flour

½ teaspoon salt

½ teaspoon cinnamon

½ teaspoon ground cloves

½ teaspoon ground nutmeg

1 teaspoon baking powder

1 cup freshly chopped walnuts

Preheat oven to 350°F.

In a small bowl, mix the persimmon pulp and baking soda and let sit; it will become gelatinous.

Meanwhile, cream the butter and sugar in a mixer until pale yellow. Add persimmon pulp and blend; it will look streaked in the butter.

Add egg, then vanilla, stirring to mix. In a separate bowl put the flour, salt, cinnamon, cloves, nutmeg, and baking powder and mix. Stir in the persimmon batter. Add the walnuts and stir.

Drop cookies onto ungreased baking sheets with a teaspoon, about 2 inches apart. Bake until just a little golden around the edges and no longer glistening on top, about 10 minutes. Be sure not to overbake. Remove from the oven and cool on racks.

Note: I always add a little extra cinnamon and nutmeg if I'm not grinding them fresh. Always be careful adding more cloves, which can be ruinous. In fact, I wouldn't do it. These cookies are really easy and very tasty, but they are so moist that they don't stack well. So, if you want them for company, try to lay them out rather than stacking.

LESLIE DANIELS

Literary Agent

Cooking is an act of seduction. You are plotting to draw someone's appetite out, to bring them to the table, even if it is yourself and toasted cheese. Nowadays, my cooking involves feeding children, but it is still seduction—perhaps even more so.

A lot of what I think about in cooking and feeding differs from my premotherhood days. Now I think more about speed and timing, more about recognizability. No mooshed foods; the best gift for a four-year-old is a pair of Eating Tweezers, to pick the broccoli out from its terrible proximity to the grain of rice. I think about nutrition and palatability, not for my own taste buds, which like bitter and acidic foods—vinegar and grapefruit—but for a milder palate. My kids are not wrong to prefer sweet ketchup to tart tomatoes. They will evolve if unforced; I tell myself this weekly. And I work on building their palates with a range of foods and a minimum of processed food with its weird, nonfood taste.

One strength I cultivate as a cook is responding to the individuality of people's tastes. There are four in our family, two kids and two parents, and I very often make a different dinner for each person. Not wholly separate dinners, but I know that the dad likes meat and could care less about potatoes; and that the tiniest person, our three-year-old daughter, refuses to chew meat and eats only potatoes, and that our son, who is six years old, solidly likes variety. He's always interested in new foods; he won't necessarily eat them, but he'll give them a good shot. My family isn't nutty, they just have different needs—we all do. I like to figure out what people like to eat, want to eat, need to eat, and cook to that.

What I try to do with my kids when I feed them is to make the meal an event where they feel they are responded to as individuals, their needs taken into account. My son and his friend spent the day together yesterday. I fed them three times in six hours—about the right amount for super-active kids. The food was simple—tuna salad, ravioli, shrimp with dip—but the message was not. The message to my son and his friend was: I want you to have a good experience at the table. I will work to make you happy, satisfied, comfortable. My daughter ate only apples, the edges of the ravioli, and no shrimp. The visitor ate everything in sight. It charmed me.

My kids have their own bowls, and I set a place for them, and I try and give them several different dishes at the same time, so if they want to eat their fruit before their meat or pasta, that's fine with me. I never say, "Save the watermelon for dessert." I've watched them eat, and they'll eat a little watermelon, a little chicken. As they get older, I'm hoping we'll all sit around as a family. Right now, their dad can hardly stand to watch them eat because they're so little and messy and dinner is not sufficiently peaceful, so it is just the three of us. But in my family growing up, we always had dinner together every night, and it provided a wonderful feeling of coming together and belonging.

At the table, I look for at least one thing that is layered with care and time: a green tomato chutney, a stew, perfectly diced vegetables. It draws your eye, your palate; there is weight to it. I also like celebratory food, when you sit down and there is a sense of occasion. It may happen in your everyday life, but it doesn't necessarily, and you should not expect it from your children because you will be disappointed, and it is better to be disappointed about things other than eating. I think people get into very difficult situations with their kids around food, and it is a complete mistake. I've seen in my own children that they really were born with different palates.

They have different tastes in what they like to eat. I don't cater to it entirely, but neither do I tell them that *this* food is right and *that* is what they should have.

My daughter really likes sweet food, and for months, she has been carrying around a basketful of plastic Easter eggs, some of which still have a few candies in them. She has been shepherding these eggs, and yes, they are beautiful and colorful, but they are also associated in her mind with sweetness. My son has still got his Halloween candy; he couldn't care less about it. I keep track of these things, and he's eaten exactly three pieces of Halloween candy since he brought it home. It's almost time to give it out for next Halloween. Both of them are on the thin side—they look like old-fashioned kids, with big heads. Both of them will eat the fat off things. They take cod liver oil, which is not to everyone's taste, but they're happy to have it. If allowed, my daughter will eat butter plain, from the stick. I will give her little pieces to eat, and I give them both a fair amount of freedom. One of the rules I've figured out in feeding children is not to make rules about food. You will think, He can't stand vegetables, and the next time at dinner you won't give him any salad, and then he'll eat the salad off your plate. If he says, "Oh, I don't eat that," ignore it. The main thing with kids is to be flexible and able to shift gears quickly. Children have the dignity not to obsess about food, unlike adults.

Cooking, for me, has its roots in play. My own mother was very, very generous about a lot of things, but especially about letting me cook with her. She set up a little square wooden table in the middle of our big old kitchen, and while she cooked, so did my sister and I, messing around. Whatever my mother was using, we could use. I can't think of another mother who would do that. My mother would let us mix things together and put them in the oven to see what would happen. I remember my sister and her friend Ruthie, who is now married to a chef, making tuna salad with cut-up bread in it. And I thought at the time, This is really a poorly organized tuna sandwich. They thought it was good and interesting. The stuff I made mostly came out like bad scrambled eggs, with sugar in it, and some other kind of sweetener—I was big on molasses—and then some flour.

Kids like to make their own food. Any tool will do: waffle iron, melon baller, apple peeler, blender. I think many more kids would like to cook if nobody told them exactly how to do it, if nobody was standing over them saying, "Oh, don't do it like that, you're going to spill." My mother wasn't like that, so we were really able to experiment—imitating her, we thought. A lot of people get very concerned about mess and waste, and it's hard not to. But if you can tame that in yourself, your kids will have a much better time. My parents are psychologists, and their idea about children is that you pay very close attention to what they call their "affect," which is really just what the child's mood is. The mood, the positive feeling, is what you preserve at all costs. If there was a mess, they didn't focus on the mess. If there were eggs being wasted, they didn't focus on the eggs being wasted. They focused on the kids having an interesting and great time. And we did; we had a fabulously good time. I think if people are allowed to explore, they can have a sense of discovery about themselves that's very gratifying: "Oh, *this* is who I am. *This* is what I like." People define themselves by the things they like, and as a child, you get information in a very primal way from eating. My mother allowed me to peel everything. I think other parents might have found that appalling. But I peeled grapes, I peeled roast beef, I peeled pound cake. My daughter does the same thing. We had doughnuts the other day, and she managed to eat the glaze off hers and give me this nude dough ring back. I have never seen anything like it.

When I was growing up, at least where we lived in Philadelphia, people didn't eat out—there wasn't take-out and carry-in and delivery and restaurants. So everything we ate, except for the occasional school lunch, was prepared by my mom. My mother is very English in her food preferences. She grew up in the Midwest, so the apex of taste for her is a shortbread cookie: butter, sugar, a little salt. She's come pretty far from that over the years, but she still thinks that anything fishy is disgusting. Give her some sole with a little bit of butter on it and that's as close to the sea as she gets—real Episcopal cooking. My mother doesn't think of herself as a good cook, although she's really an excellent cook. She was—is—an intellectual, and throughout her life her ideas formed her approach to everything, even food. She was very concerned about nutrition. She made a lot of stewed fruit, things that I thought were barely passable as dessert, but she was very creative about it. There was one summertime dessert she would make with green grapes in an ice cube tray, sprinkled with brown sugar and covered with sour cream, and put it in the refrigerator for the afternoon. It was a fabulous combination of flavors; the brown sugar would melt into the sour cream.

Growing up, I was mostly interested in baking because that seemed like the only way I was going to get sweets. Our house was in the city, but we had a sour cherry tree in the backyard. My grandmother would come every summer around cherry harvest, and we'd make sour cherry pies. That is some kind of pinnacle of American culinary delight: sour cherry pie, with vanilla ice cream if you want. My grandmother would also make watermelon pickle, which is another good old-style American thing that you don't see anymore. She would bring a dark, molassesy-looking brine with cloves and allspice to a boil; we'd peel the green off the watermelon, and eat the pink, and soak the white in the brine for a couple of weeks. This recipe may have been from her grandmother, who was from Marietta, Georgia, but came north just prior to the Civil War.

I loved cooking with my grandmother; she was a great storyteller. She had not only stories about her childhood but also little rhymes for when you had snarls in your hair, and for when you had a booboo on your knee. She was a Victorian. She came from a time when you had to entertain children; you couldn't just plug them into a video. She was raised in an aristocratic milieu, and she wasn't taught to cook, only to play the organ and make wonderful conversation. I think much of motherhood and being a wife came as a series of awful surprises to her.

So I don't see my mother at her mother's knee, learning how to cook. I think she taught herself. She had some cookbooks, like those of Adele Davis who, may she rest in peace, had terrible taste buds. Wholesome ideas about nutrition, Ms. Davis, but she would put some really disgusting things together, and there was always liver in there somewhere, which is hard for kids to eat, and it is not easy for grown-ups, either. Since my mother didn't style herself a great cook, I was never aware so much of apprenticing myself to her, but I certainly learned a lot of confidence from her that she probably doesn't feel about herself. She believed in my sister and me, which is an incredible gift to give your kids. Because of that confidence, I've always felt like I could take on any recipe.

I find it peculiar that people consider cooking to be an option or a hobby. To me, it's so integrated with living and caring for yourself. Even when I was a single career girl (which I carried on for decades), I always cooked, although not in any elaborate way. I tend to improvise well on soups. I'd come home from work and have a bowl of soup and a piece of bread and a piece of fruit, and that was dinner, and then I'd go to bed. I was never very organized about it, but I would make a pot of soup and eat it for a few days, and share it or not. I find that my health is completely tied up with feeding myself, and I like catering to exactly what I want. Should I have spinach, I want to have a little butter in it; I don't want to have half a cup of grease, which is how a lot of restaurants, even good restaurants, treat foods—with a lot of fat, a lot of salt, and a good amount of sugar. It's not wholesome. The biggest legacy my mom gave me is the feeling of this is what real food tastes like, and this is what it feels like in your body.

It takes a fair amount of energy to care for yourself; it's sort of like being your own mother and saying, "This is what we're going to do, and we're going to do it every day." I went to college when I was fifteen years old, and I wasn't prepared, then, to feed myself. It was sort of a deranging experience, because I thought I could cook but I really couldn't. I could make scrambled eggs and toast and that was about it. Beyond that, though, I don't think you can take care of yourself every day when you're that age. I didn't starve; I went to school in my hometown, so I would often go to my parents' and eat a lot of food that would last me for a couple of days. I'm sure my mother tried to send food to school with me, but there's a lot of organization that goes into cooking for yourself that I just didn't have at that time. It came naturally as I was able to take more responsibility for myself, and it probably came in part from taking care of other people. I had a very early marriage, in which I was a stepmom. With kids, you have to feed them—often. And since *not* cooking was never modeled for me, it never occurred to me that I wouldn't have to cook. Plus, I've always liked it. I've always felt that it was very grounding. It's a translation of your feelings for people and a gathering of energies for any group, but particularly a family.

I cooked at nineteen, just out of university, living on the West Coast for the first time. I fed my friends, offering myself in a way that I was unable to do in conversations: "Here, eat, taste, get me? See?" My dear friend Rosa and I made "fast food" slowly: egg rolls with duck sauce. The duck sauce base was home-canned apricots from her great-aunt's tree, blended with dry mustard, fresh garlic, and I don't remember what else, maybe a splash of tamari. It was the perfect color, and delicious. Rosa taught me how to deep-fry. I have not done it since, nor am I likely to start, but the egg rolls with fresh shrimp, bean sprouts, and bok choy were marvelous. It was the opposite of fast food, taking us all afternoon to chop, cook, serve, as our friends gathered and talked. Later, that group of friends splintered apart with marriages and divorces, babies born, and fallings out, but at that point we gathered around a table, laughing and eating in one prime of our lives.

I have a friend who's a writer, and married to a writer, and she came and had dinner with me recently. She said, "My husband won't go to people's houses if they aren't good cooks; he won't put himself in the position of sitting at a table with bad food and not eating it." I thought that was funny. You have to work hard to make bad food. My first marriage came with a mother-in-law, and she could kill you with her mysterious middle-European food that expanded in your stomach once you'd eaten it; it just got bigger and bigger. I think cooking is more about the cook than it is about the eater. When people cook for you, they're giving you a piece of themselves. It's friendship, but also, as with any kind of creation you're putting yourself into, you're saying, "Here I am; this is for you."

I can go to the refrigerator and look in it and improvise a dinner where not that many people could come up with something. Condiments are good. Anchovies, say, with one fresh tomato and a good vinegar. I went through a long mustard phase. At the moment, I like miso, and I like mango chutney. I think miso and mango chutney can make a lot of stuff more interesting than it deserves to be. I've been making, I guess you'd call it, a barbecue-taste chicken with miso. Miso's great in salad dressings. Mango chutney you can have with a frittata. Very often for lunch, I'll have a bowl of rice with some sort of leftover meat, and mango chutney can work well on those informal occasions. I often feel like I'm eating some sort of ethnic or tribal cuisine, but I have no idea what it is.

I recently moved from the city to a small town in a fairly rural area. That adjustment had to be accompanied by another kind of shift; I couldn't take my city ways and make them work here. This also goes for food. I bought a church potluck-supper cookbook and I was reading it before I went to sleep and thinking, Sheet cake—that's what you make here when you need something for a bake sale. You don't take designer muffins and try to adapt them; you cook differently. I used to think, What the heck are casseroles? Because they weren't part of my experience. But we had a very long winter this year, and for my children's father, casseroles are somehow a very central idea of comfort and family. I was determined to find casseroles for him. So I flipped through my Marcella Hazan–type cookbooks for casserole recipes and forget about it. But then I found the church supper cookbook and I made shepherd's pie–type casseroles from it, and cottage pies. And then I realized, This is just the thing.

Also this winter, I was involved in a committee that was putting on a book festival, and there were a number of meetings, and I cooked for them. These were always lunchtime meetings, because everyone's kids would be in school then, and the committee was comprised of moms. It was incredibly gratifying to cook for mothers who don't get cooked for, or who don't like to cook at all, or who are tired of cooking. They are often most grateful and surprised by someone offering them healthful and satisfying food: soup with vegetables and rice, fruit salad with hulled strawberries, a green salad sprinkled with pumpkin seeds and dressed with thirty-second homemade salad dressing.

I have some unofficial guidelines, broken constantly, having to do with my desire to cook both well and appropriately, and to save time:

- Be irreverent about food and cooking.

- Cook what you have in the house; let that be your discipline.

- Cook the vegetables as soon as you can: roast them, sauté dark greens, make squash into soup and tomatoes into bisque. Make these things some

Sunday, or even at ten A.M. when you return from the market. Then, on a rushed evening, you can serve a good dinner with five minutes' preparation: heat soup, tear lettuce, toss on the salad some roasted vegetables, or a wedge of cheese, a sprinkle of seeds or nuts or beans, or cooked chicken or hard-boiled egg. Croutons (toast a piece of bread twice, cube). Eat. This method also saves you from organic-broccoli guilt: that forgotten six-dollar head of broccoli turning to compost in the back of the fridge.

- When you feel edgy, make a pot of rice. I always feel that if you don't know what to do to take care of yourself, you should make rice. The rest of the world lives on it. You can get along on a pot of rice if you're a career girl or a lost soul. Make a pot of rice and it will get you through a few days.

- When you feel undeserving, bake something—a loaf of cornbread will do nicely.

Feed yourself!

Recipes for Children

• CORN CHOWDER •

This is adapted from the White Dog Café Cookbook *by Judy Wicks, Kevin von Klaus, Elizabeth Fitzgerald, and Mardee Haidin Regan—that is, I took out all the extra spicing to make it palatable to my children. But my parents like it, too. The flavor is helped a lot by very fresh corn.*

Serves 4

5 or 6 ears raw corn
1 small onion, minced

2 tablespoons butter

Bacon (optional)

1 heaping tablespoon flour

1 (14 ounce) can chicken stock

2½ cups milk

Use a sharp knife to cut the kernels from the corn cobs into a large bowl. After you've cut off the kernels, scrape the cob with a butter knife or spoon.

In a soup pot over medium heat sauté the onion in butter. (You may also sauté a small amount of bacon.) When the onion is translucent, sprinkle with the flour and continue to cook for several minutes. Stir some to discourage lumps.

Add the corn. Cook for another 5 minutes over low to moderate heat, stirring occasionally.

Add the stock. Simmer for a few minutes to heat the soup.

Add the milk. Heat through but do not boil. Serve immediately.

• ROASTED VEGETABLES •

The main point in cooking for your children, after the obvious ones of taste and nutrition, is to spend the minimum amount of time possible in preparation. There is a 50 percent chance they will reject what you've made and it is demoralizing if you have invested real time in it. Here is my answer to French fries.

Serves 4

¼ cup olive oil

4 medium-sized Yukon gold potatoes, scrubbed and quartered

Salt

Ketchup (optional)

Preheat oven to 375°F.

Pour olive oil into a shallow roasting pan (a cookie sheet with edges will do).

Put cut Yukon gold potatoes in the pan with the oil (other kinds work, but these are lovely). Any size slices will do but keep it uniform. Salt lightly if desired. Toss with a spatula to distribute the oil.

Roast for 45 minutes, turning once. Serve with ketchup, if you like.

VARIATIONS:

Many vegetables will work: carrots, sweet potatoes, zucchini, eggplant, onions. Each will take different amounts of time to cook, so pierce them with a sharp knife to test for doneness.

· BREAD PUDDING: FAST VERSION ·

Serves 4

6 to 8 slices leftover bread, cubed (the bread can be stale)

½ cup raisins

3 eggs

1½ cups butter, plus more for greasing the pan

1 teaspoon vanilla

¼ cup maple syrup

Nutmeg

Preheat oven to 325°F. Butter the inside of a 1-quart soufflé dish.

Place the bread in the baking pan or soufflé dish. Add the raisins, unless your kid picks them out. In a small bowl, beat the eggs. Add the milk, vanilla, maple syrup, and a couple of scrapes of nutmeg. Stir and pour over the bread. Soak for a few minutes.

Bake for about 35 minutes. When it is done, the pudding will puff up and turn light brown. The center may still be slightly liquid but not runny.

Remove from the oven. Serve warm.

- Here is an alternate (maybe more satisfying) use for stale bread. Keep a bag in the fridge or freezer to add crusts, heels, and forgotten pieces. When you have plenty, defrost and go feed the ducks, birds, gulls, fish, or squirrels.

- Here are some other dessert ideas that are so simple they can't be called recipes. But my mother used to feed them to us and we thought they were "dessert."

  1. Sliced bananas sprinkled with wheat germ and brown sugar, with milk
  2. Berries with milk or cream and a sprinkle of sugar
  3. Frozen grapes (seedless)
  4. Almost any fruit, peeled. The ceremony of peeling a fruit and offering it to a child (or grown-up) makes it special.

ACKNOWLEDGMENTS

Any time I write anything at all, I find myself indebted to battalions of gracious, generous people who emerge, sometimes seemingly out of nowhere, when they are least expected, to offer support and inspiration in ways both practical and mystical. This book is certainly no exception. I am almost unutterably grateful to the fifteen women whose lives fill these pages. For their time, their effort, and their enthusiasm, I am so deeply obliged. Without the mothers—Leslie Daniels, Kristina Salen, and Gab Casper especially—who understood how it was that in the first year of my daughter's life I should be so in need of encouragement, and gave it, I would never have found my way through to the far side of this project. Every new mother should be so lucky in her friends.

Noel, Sean, Donna, and Brooke at St. Helen fed my gossip and caffeine monkeys, making it almost impossible for me to get any work done at their café. But distraction and procrastination are often a writer's best friends. And finally, I am beholden for all time to my editor and dear friend, Sara Carder, for, well, *everything*; to Denver Butson, Rhonda Keyser, and Maybelle Lorraine, just because; and to Rob, for loving me anyway.

RESOURCES

To learn more about the women in this book and the things that interest them, see the following:

PANKTI SEVAK

South Asian Women's Network: www.sawnet.org
Flavorful India: Treasured Recipes from a Gujarati Family by Priti Chitni Gress

MAYA KAIMAL

www.mayakaimal.com

TESSA HUXLEY

Community Food Security Coalition: www.foodsecurity.org
American Community Gardening Association: www.communitygardening.org

ANNA LAPPÉ

Hope's Edge: The Next Diet for a Small Planet by Frances Moore Lappé and Anna Lappé
Small Planet Fund: www.smallplanetfund.org

CHARLOTTE GOULD

Mothers Across America: www.mothersacrossamerica.com

KENDALL CROLIUS

American Cancer Society's Relay for Life: find the link through www.cancer.org

NANCY BUTCHER

Beauty by Nancy Butcher

At Home with Japanese Cooking by Elizabeth Andoh

MICHELLE LATIOLAIS

Even Now by Michelle Latiolais

LYNETTE LATIOLAIS DAVIS

The Slow Food movement: www.slowfood.com

Julia Child's kitchen at the Smithsonian Institution:
www.americanhistory.si.edu/juliachild

RECIPE INDEX